Muqaddima

of Ibn Khaldun

Book One
Chapter Five

Making a Living

by ***Abd al-Rahman Ibn Khaldun***

A New Translation
by *Ahmed E. Souaiaia*

An Institute for Integrated Systems Thinking sponsored project.

Published in the United States of America

First Published in 2023

ISBN: 979-8-88823-000-8 Hardback

ISBN: 979-8-88823-001-5 Paperback

For

the many dear family members who kindly and graciously endured my incessant quoting of Ibn Khaldun;

students in my course on wealth and inequity, who inspired this work;
and

Maggie, for bringing the translation to life.

Table of Contents

Contents

Foreword ii
The Significance of Ibn Khaldun's Thought v
Muqaddima of Ibn Khaldun, Book One, Chapter Five: 1
Making a Living 1
1. On the Origins and Meaning of Subsistence and Earnings 1
2. On Ways, Means, and Methods of Making a Living 6
3. On How Being a Servant is not a Natural Way of Making a Living 9
4. On How Seeking Money from Buried Objects and Treasures is not a Natural Way of Making a Living 12
5. On the Benefits of *Jāh* and Wealth 19
7. On Persons in Charge of Religious Affairs including Judges, Muftis, Teachers, Imams, Preachers, and Mu'azzins 28
8. On Agriculture 30
9. On Trade: Meaning, Methods, and Types 31
11. On the Ethics of Merchants 34
13. On Hoarding 37
14. On the Effects of Cheap Prices 39
15. On the Ethics of Merchants 41
16. On Acquiring *Ṣanā'i`* 43
17. On *Ṣanā'i`* and Urbanization 45
18. On what Makes *Ṣanā'i`* Established in a Country 47
19. On What Improves Quality and Quantity of *Ṣanā'i`* 49
20. On the Relation Between the Condition of a Country and *Ṣanā'i`* 50
21. On the Arabs and *Ṣanā'i`* 51
22. On Acquired Abilities 53
23. On the Hierarchy of *Ṣanā'i`* 54
24. On Agriculture 55
25. On Building 56
26. On Carpentry 62
27. On the *Ṣinā`a* of Weaving and Tailoring 64
28. On Midwifery 67
29. On Medicine 72
30. On Calligraphy and Writing 77
31. On Writing and Recordkeeping 90
32. On the *Ṣinā`a* of Singing 94
33. On the Fact that *Ṣanā'i`*, Especially Writing and Calculus, Endow its Masters with a Sharp Mind (*`aql*) 104
Glossary of Key Words and Concepts 106
Index 112

Foreword

As graduate student at the University of Washington, I took several Arabic reading courses with the late Pierre MacKay (1933–2015). Although he was retired for a while when I joined the program, he nonetheless continued to offer what was clearly his favorite course's subject matter: Reading selections from Ibn Khaldun's *Muqaddima*. His personal interest in Ibn Khaldun's thought drove him to teach this course every year despite his retirement; and I suspect that it was personal interest that drove the small number of students to take such a difficult and elective Arabic course. I, too, was driven to take a reading course on Ibn Khaldun for personal reasons: I was born in the same country Ibn Khaldun was born in (Tunisia), my ancestors came from the same country where Ibn Khaldun started to draft *al-Muqaddima* (Algeria), and the high school I attended in Tunisia was named after him.

I was told by other faculty members, friends of Prof. MacKay, that he told them that he enjoyed and appreciated having me in the class because I offered new insight about Ibn Khaldun's influence and his reliance on Berber language and cultures, which he was not familiar with as a scholar who was trained in Classical Arabic. I did not make much of that comment until I started to teach a course on wealth, inequity, and economics, for which I included few reading assignments from and about Ibn Khaldun (selections from Rosenthal's translation of *al-Muqaddima* and several secondary works engaged with Ibn Khaldun's economic thought).

Over time, reading students' writings, I noticed some common misrepresentations of Ibn Khaldun's ideas—compelling me to look for a reason for the pattern of misrepresentation. I expected the misrepresentations to be derived from secondary literature. It turned out that the translation played the major role for it not only was the only source for economists who did not know Arabic but wrote about Ibn Khaldun's economic thought, but the translation itself included interpretative statements that cannot be fully supported by the evidence in the primary sources--the final draft of *al-Muqaddima* and the published Arabic volumes currently in circulation. That is when I decided to take a close look at the Arabic text and compare it to Rosenthal's translation of *al-Muqaddima*, which lead me to believe that new translations of *al-Muqaddima*, not just my translation, should be produced in order to introduce the possible range of ideas contained in such complex work. I started with the section on *ma'āsh*, mainly to offer my students an alternative translation.

I hope that the rest of al-Muqaddima will be translated as well and I hope that more scholars will do the same, for Ibn Khaldun's thought is quite rich, complex, difficult, and, importantly, relevant.

Ahmed E. Souaiaia, University of Iowa, Iowa City, IA, USA.

September 15, 2023.

The Significance of Ibn Khaldun's Thought[1]

Most modern scholars who engage with Ibn Khaldun's work consider him a social historian whose work is useful in that it sheds light on events and institutions they wish to reference. For these scholars researching in languages other than Arabic, translations of Ibn Khaldun often serve as their source material from which to draw conclusions. Yet a close comparison between the original Arabic text of his seminal work, *al-Muqaddima*, and some of the English-language secondary sources that have drawn conclusions from it, reveals some misinterpretations. As a corrective counterweight and drawing from the Arabic text of *al-Muqaddima*, this work highlights Ibn Khaldun's reliance on systems thinking and his original ideas in relation to some of the most consequential areas of social activities and human behaviors. This article avoids the reductionist approach that focuses on a single idea, imposing it as being Ibn Khaldun's unique original contribution, but, instead, tracks with key ideas as Ibn Khaldun presents them in Part 5, Book 1 of his *Muqaddima*'s section on economic systems and values.

Readers might benefit from an outline of this work so that they are better able to contextualize its content and understand its reasons for including or excluding certain topics and subjects. An outline might also help direct readers' attentions to specific areas of interest and the key ideas that shape Ibn Khaldun's worldview, which this author believes many English-language secondary works have omitted.

This article is divided into four main sections: brief comments on the secondary works that have interpreted and presented Ibn Khaldun's thought, notes on the function of translation and its impact on secondary works of scholarship, a textual analysis of Ibn Khaldun's economic philosophy based on an analytical reading of the original Arabic texts, and a list of what this author considers the most significant contributions of Ibn Khaldun along with recommendations for possible future research undertakings.

[1] Adapted from *Reading and interpreting Ibn Khaldun's economic philosophy*, published in The Journal of Philosophical Economics, 2023.

In this work, sample statements from the English translation of Ibn Khaldun's work and the secondary works that have engaged with Ibn Khaldun's thought underscore the need for both more translations and more secondary works that engage with their primary sources rather than relying on a single translation. If the original Arabic text is available in at least ten different editions, and given the potential variance among these Arabic editions, is it not reasonable to expect the production of many translations as well, to reflect not only the variance in Ibn Khaldun's manuscripts and subsequent published book editions but, importantly, the variance that must occur when translating from one language to another?

The section on translations and secondary works replaces the usual literature review of scholarship in academic papers because, in this case, the quality of such literature and their source materials (a single translation) merits questioning. Therefore, it stands to reason that this paper should allocate energy and space to direct engagements with the Arabic texts of the original work of Ibn Khaldun, rather than engage at length with allegedly deficient content.

Moreover, some secondary works present Ibn Khaldun's ideas as unoriginal and nonconsequential. It would benefit the scholarly community to highlight Ibn Khaldun's ideas that are significant and consequential and expand the conversation on Ibn Khaldun's contribution to social theories and economic philosophy, rather than merely focus on secondary literature that lacks sufficiently diverse perspectives and sources. Given that some readers of Ibn Khaldun's work are skeptical of the level of originality and depth of his contributions, this article highlights what this author considers the compelling and consequential propositions that might have shaped Ibn Khaldun's worldview in relations to economic activity, wealth distribution, and systems of values, ethics, politics, and social behavior.

It is reasonable to ask for the impetus for connecting translation, interpretation, and exploration of a foreign language work in an article limited by space and structural considerations. Therefore, a few comments justifying such a connection are in order.

The purpose of the brief comments on the translation and some of its problems is to underscore the importance of translation as an interpretive undertaking that is connected to secondary theoretical works, for translation bridges primary sources and secondary literature, thus guiding and influencing subsequent scholars' interpretations and findings. There is no neutral translation. A translation reflects the methodological, disciplinary, cultural, and political biases of the translator. Therefore, theoretical works critiquing and recasting a foreign language text benefit from a plurality of translations produced by individuals from different backgrounds.

Secondary works that are based on a single translation, and which then become a source for other secondary works, risk degrading the connection to their primary source materials. It is critical that authors of secondary works are mindful of the biases of their interpretations and theories, and that they disclose their level of engagement with original sources.

With the above concerns in mind, it becomes clear that one can reconstruct Ibn Khaldun's thought through a comprehensive reading of his work relevant to all connected systems described and analyzed in the primary source materials. Secondary works of scholarship would benefit substantively and conceptually from the availability of additional translations of Ibn Khaldun's work, not just the abundance of secondary interpretive works that might be based on a single translation.

The above concerns guide the framing of this article and define its scope. The aim of this work is to engage directly with Ibn Khaldun's original texts on economic and social philosophy. To that end, this work addresses the following questions: What are the most consequential ideas of Ibn Khaldun's economic thought? What theoretical framework might have guided his reasoning? And which topics and ideas merit further discussions and analysis? The answers to these questions are rooted in a holistic analysis of related ideas beyond those found in the chapter on economic activities and schemes—*ma'āsh*.

Situating and interpreting Ibn Khaldun

Ibn Khaldun* may have been the last Islamic thinker who understood and interpreted the world without any measure of influence from the profusion of Western ideas and events that shaped modern civilization.[2] He was one of the most original and provocative, yet nonconsequential, social historians and political thinkers, in large part because he lived at a singular moment in history: at the seam of the Islamic and Western civilizations. As he predicted, Islamic civilization had reached a stage of decline, and there was no single strategic thinker who could have reversed the course of its historical trajectory at that point. Therefore, Ibn Khaldun's contribution should not be assessed the same way as Renaissance and Enlightenment thinkers' contributions: by how much influence they had on their contemporary and successive leaders and thinkers.

Enlightenment thinkers promoted reason as the means through which to address the absolutism of religious institutions and emphasized life, liberty, and property to resist the tyranny of monarchies and authoritarian rulers. As an event, Enlightenment marked the beginning of discovery and progress for modern Western societies.

Ibn Khaldun, on the other hand, understood that the Golden Age of the Islamic civilization, which started at the end of the 8th century (CE), had reached its end when the Mongol invasion collapsed the seat of the Abbasid Caliphate in 1258 CE. Although the Islamic dynasties in North Africa (Maghreb; west) and the Iberian Peninsula (Andalus; Andalusia) were insulated from the effects of the struggles of the Islamic dynasties in the east due to their autonomous status, their internal strife tied their fate to the inertia of the declining civilization that represented all Muslims.

These radically different circumstances and conditions of the Western world and the Islamic world of that time placed Ibn Khaldun in a unique position that must be factored in when interpreting his thought and reconstructing his worldview, especially in relation to the political and philosophical economy. Ibn Khaldun's contributions ought to be weighed by the quality of knowledge that he passed on and the utility of predictions derived from his knowledge; for he lived on the edge of human transition from one extraordinarily volatile era, marked by decline of the civilization of which he was a member to another rising civilization about which

[2] By the close of 1900 CE, scholars had cited Ibn Khaldun about 50 times. However, most entries were references to historical events mentioned in Ibn Khaldun's work. Prior to the 20th century, no major work engaged with his theoretical contribution. Since the start of the 20th century, on the other hand, scholars have referenced Ibn Khaldun about 9,000 times. In contrast: Thomas Aquinas has been cited about 90,000 times; René Descartes, 50,000; Immanuel Kant, 80,000; and Emile Durkheim, to whom Ibn Khaldun is often compared, 45,000 scholarly references.

he has knowledge and that he did not include in his presentation of social history.

Moreover, in academia, originality is a modern standard, one that lacks humility one might add; it is not a universal standard that cuts across cultures and times. Ibn Khaldun would have judged his own work and the works of his peers by their depth and breadth of knowledge, not by the appropriation of an accretive body of knowledge augmented by many thinkers and scholars from different communities and different time periods.

Considering the fact that the Renaissance signaled a robust interest in investigating previous cultures' most significant contributions to art, architecture, astronomy, science and literature, and given that Ibn Khaldun, as his work testifies, was engaged in collecting and cataloging human advances in these same areas of knowledge, it is curious that Western Renaissance thinkers did not give his work the same attention or make it the subject of interest in the same way they justified their interest in Greek and Roman cultures. This omission becomes even more curious given the fact that Ibn Khaldun produced his seminal works during the same period when Renaissance thinkers started on their journey of rediscovering the legacy of ancient civilizations, around the 14th century CE.

Later generations of scholars, including Enlightenment thinkers and beyond, did not rectify Renaissance thinkers' exclusion of Ibn Khaldun's work from the processes of exploring ancient classics. It was not until the emergence of Orientalist scholars in the 20th century that thinkers began attempting to translate and engage with Ibn Khaldun's thought.

Still, in the context of modern Western scholarship on the Islamic civilization and the emerging academic area of study broadly known as 'Islamic studies,' Ibn Khaldun should be the most studied classical Islamic thinker. Yet, little consensus—through scholarly assessments of his theoretical framework, and particularly its originality and significance—has emerged about the nature of his work. The few works Orientalist scholars who have produced regarding Ibn Khaldun are more focused on discrediting his thought than on conducting a substantive examination of his work.

For instance, after embarking on review of previous works of scholarship that might have influenced Ibn Khaldun, a twentieth century Orientalist scholar found that Ibn Khaldun's claim to originality is, at best, disappointing. The review's author argued that, notwithstanding any direct link between Ibn Khaldun's work to works of previous thinkers, we should not assume his ideas are his: 'In what measure Ibn Khaldun was influenced by the writings of the authors just passed in review, or by others, is hard to determine.' Nonetheless, because some of the ideas he touched upon were 'widely held (having been effectively treated in Plato's political works) and must have been known to Ibn Khaldun' (Spengler 1964, p.283), the Orientalist author argues, no measure of originality should be granted to Ibn Khaldun. Some Orientalist scholars are even willing to credit Ibn Khaldun's ideas to 15th-century Fürstenspiegel literature (Spengler 1964, p.283), a post-Ibn Khaldun development, rather concede that Ibn Khaldun had contributed original ideas that progressed thinking. In the view of these scholars, what Ibn Khaldun did was cobble together a framework out of 'bits and details' (Spengler 1964, p.283), not produce a coherent, congruent, original work of scholarship.

Secondary literature that engaged with Ibn Khaldun's thought were shallow, uninformed, and rooted in conjectures perhaps due to personal bias or lack of a linguistic capacity and competence that would have allowed their authors to skillfully parse and analyze Ibn Khaldun's complex thinking. By these authors' consistent reference to the translation, it is evident that the secondary literature Orientalists produced relied heavily on the assumptions and conjectures of translators to craft and support their own conjecture-based assessments of Ibn Khaldun's ideas. Economist Joseph J. Spengler, for instance, asserts that it 'remains true, however, that [Ibn Khaldun] knew or drew on many sources, among them Fürstenspiegel and administrative writings' (Spengler 1964, p.283). This statement that Ibn Khaldun's source material is uncontested fact—that what he used as sources 'remains true'—is not, in itself, a finding based on facts. It comes from on another assumption, which Ibn Khaldun's translator, Franz Rosenthal, proposed:

> We should perhaps be justified in assuming that practically every matter of detail found in the *Muqaddimah* was probably not original with Ibn Khaldun, but had been previously expressed elsewhere. Even his characterization of *`asabiyah* as a positive factor in society, or his demand for knowledge of social conditions as prerequisite to the historian's correct evaluation of historical information, although seemingly

original ideas, may have been inspired by a source yet to be rediscovered. (Rosenthal 1958, p.854; Spengler 1964, p.283)[3]

Such poor grasp of Ibn Khaldun's nuanced and technical formulation of ideas was evident in the way Orientalist scholars understood and presented their interpretation of Ibn Khaldun's main theory, which in their view is related to the cyclicity of civilization. They opined that 'civilization and culture,' as Ibn Khaldun presents them, 'had moved somewhat cyclically, fluctuating between nomadism and sedentary civilizations' (Spengler 1964, p.289). Moreover, scholars who engaged with the translation of Ibn Khaldun's work saw his ideas as limited and applicable only to the cultures and communities with which he was familiar—those of Spain and North Africa. Some modern Western scholars explicitly denied that Ibn Khaldun 'apprehended or intended so universal a model' based on his 'cultural fluctuation' (Spengler 1964, p.289) theory.

Either because of the flaws in the translation, or because of their failure to appreciate Ibn Khaldun's careful and deliberate choice of words to discuss technical matters, Orientalist scholars collapse Ibn Khaldun's categories into a single conceptual framework. They erroneously see his reference to *`umrān* and *ḥaḍāra* as using two different words to refer to the same thing: culture. The cyclical theory, which Orientalists see as the only semi-original idea that Ibn Khaldun contributed, is—in their understandings—rooted in his 'concern with "civilization" (*`umrān*), or culture' (Spengler 1964, p.294).[4]

It is important to note that most secondary works on Ibn Khaldun draw heavily, if not exclusively, from a single translation of *al-Muqaddima,* which has not been significantly revised since it was first published more than half a century ago (Rosenthal 1958). At first glance, the lack of other translations of all or parts of *al-*

---

[3] From Franz Rosenthal's commentary on *al-Muqaddima*; a fuller quote than the one cited by Spengler, 283.

[4] See also Dale, Stephen Frederic (2006), "Ibn Khaldun: The Last Greek and the First Annaliste Historian." *International Journal of Middle East Studies*, vol. 38, no. 3, pp. 431–51; Gibb, H. A. R. (1933), "The Islamic Background of Ibn Khaldun's Political Theory." *Bulletin of the School of Oriental Studies*, University of London, vol. 7, no. 1, pp. 23–31; Rosen, Lawrence (2005), "Theorizing from within: Ibn Khaldun and His Political Culture." *Contemporary Sociology*, vol. 34, no. 6, pp. 596–99; Jean David C. Boulakia. "Ibn Khaldûn: A Fourteenth-Century Economist." *Journal of Political Economy*, vol. 79, no. 5, 1971, pp. 1105–18; Gellner, Ernest (1975), "Cohesion and Identity: The Maghreb from Ibn Khaldun to Emile Durkheim." *Government and Opposition*, vol. 10, no. 2, 203–18; and de Muijnck, Sam, et al. (2021), "History of Economic Thought & Methods." *Economy Studies: A Guide to Rethinking Economics Education, Amsterdam University Press*, 187–99.

Muqaddima might suggest that Rosenthal's original translation was adequate and authoritative enough to render producing a new translation redundant and unnecessary. To evaluate these assumptions, we must review not only some of secondary literature, but, importantly, the translation of Ibn Khaldun's *Muqaddima* that non-Arabic literate scholars have used, comment generally on translation as an interpretive activity, and present an alternative translation to the sections on economic thought and events. Here, the goal is to highlight some of Ibn Khaldun's theoretical ideas, especially those distinguishable from related ideas driving modern institutions and informing the modern discourses in a number of critical areas of public life.

The functions of translation in relation to primary sources

Examining the body of secondary literature that introduces and interprets Ibn Khaldun's economic ideas reveals a curious pattern: The English secondary works that relied exclusively on the English translation share the same understanding, assessment, and critiques; whereas the English secondary works that relied on the Arabic only, or on the English translation and the Arabic works, are divergent and diverse in terms of their understandings, assessments, and critiques of Ibn Khaldun's ideas. This pattern alone, ironic in its notable unoriginality, was compelling enough for this author to take a closer look at the English translation and compare it to the Arabic text. However, needing to research and answer many serious questions from students about Ibn Khaldun's ideas made it imperative that more primary sources are examined, including the Arabic work—*al-Muqaddima*.[5] In doing so, it was discovered that in addition to substantive differences resulting from the variance among the slightly different manuscripts and/or editions of the Arabic text, there were also serious errors with word choice and, in many cases, missteps with basic understanding of the North African Arabic dialect that influenced Ibn Khaldun's writing. To illustrate the nature of the problems with Rosenthal's translation, it would suffice to point out just one example.

[5] *Muqaddimat Ibn Khaldun*, often abbreviated as *al-Muqaddima*, is the first volume of Ibn Khaldun's history with the Arabic title, *Diwan al-mubtada' wa-l-khabar fi tarikh al-`arab wa-l-barbar waman `asarahum min thawi al-sha'n al-akbar*. The Arabic text and this author's translation relied on and cross-referenced the Moroccan edition, *al-Muqaddima*, the Lebanese edition, *Muqaddimat Ibn Khaldun*,, the Egyptian edition, *Muqaddimat Ibn Khaldun*, the Tunisian edition, *Kitab al-`ibar wa-diwan al-mubtada' wa-l-khabar fi tarikh al-`arab wa-l-barbar waman `asarahum min thawi al-sha'n al-akbar*, and the Syrian edition, *Muqaddimat Ibn Khaldun*.

In part five (*al-bāb al- ḳāmis*) of book one (*al-kitāb al-awwal*), covering economic themes, Ibn Khaldun defines trade (*tijāra*) this way:

> *i`lam anna al-tijārata muḥāwalatu al-kasbi bi-tanmiyati al-māli bi-shirā'i al-sila`i bi-'l-ruḳṣi wa-bay`ihā bi-al-ġalā'i ay-yama kānati al-sil`atu min daqīqin 'aw zar`in 'aw ḥayawānin 'aw qumāsh.* (Ibn Khaldun 2001, p.1:494)

Here is how Rosenthal translated this passage:

> It should be known that commerce means the attempt to make a profit by increasing capital, through buying goods at a low price and selling them at a high price, whether these goods consist of slaves, grain, animals, weapons, or clothing material.

Here is this author's translation:

> It should be known that trade is the attempt to earn money by augmenting capital through the buying of merchandise at a cheap price and selling it at an expensive price, whether the merchandise might it be flour, crop, animal, or fabric.

The difference between these translations is not merely disagreement over word choice in the presence of many options from many cognates—like 'trade' or 'commerce.' Rather, the difference touches on substantive additions and omissions. In the Arabic text, the list of 'goods' (*sila`*) names only four objects. Rosenthal's list consists of five objects. The difference could be attributed to the source upon which Rosenthal relied. The possibility that that the translator had access to a different manuscript or book edition that might have included those words shows the need for more critical works and for more transparency in deciding which manuscript or which edition one must rely on and what standard, if any, is used to make that decision. The same way there are numerous manuscripts (about 6 partial or full manuscripts by some accounts) and numerous published editions of *al-Muqaddima* (more than 11 editions are now available), there should be numerous translations.

Many interpreters of and commentators on Ibn Khaldun's work did not pay close attention to the fact that Ibn Khaldun relied on Maghribi Arabic. The word *daqīq* in Arabic may mean fine, detailed, or thin. However, the word *daqīq* has been used throughout the Maghrib region to refer to ground grain, or flour. Rosenthal may have preferred the single manuscript that contained *raqīq* instead of *daqīq* to avoid confusion and overcome the unusual origins of the latter word.

Western scholars are familiar with the notion that some human beings might be considered 'property.' Within Western societies, women and slaves have been considered 'property.' They also understand this to have been the case in some Arab and Islamic societies. The Qur'ān, for instance, refers to enslaved war captives as 'what your right hand possessed.'[6] It is not farfetched, then, to believe that Ibn Khaldun considered slaves to be a form of goods or merchandise (*sil`a*). He might have. But in this context, he did not. It is far more probable that he used the word for 'flour.'

In the same space, Rosenthal understood *kasb* to mean 'profit.' Ibn Khaldun is very specific and deliberate about the use of the words *kasb* and *rizq*. He coined these words to mean specific things and he used them consistently in specific contexts. Nonetheless, Rosenthal collapses Ibn Khaldun's sentence and the meanings of his words to define trade as the act of profiting from selling goods. Ibn Khaldun defines trade (*tijāra*) as a process or scheme of increasing one's wealth (*māl*). There is a clear and significant difference, as it will be explained when Ibn Khaldun's theory on the store of value, virtues of trade, and other matters related to economics are introduced in later parts of this work.

Disagreements over which cognates to use are compelling enough alone to encourage others to propose different translations of the same work. However, these diverging choices in combination with the disagreements involving personal and social bias, the lack of appreciation of the level of influence of Berber languages and cultures on Ibn Khaldun's writing, and the fact of Ibn Khaldun's highly technical language, make it imperative that scholars with diverse expertise and disciplines produce new translations of the work of one of the most important thinkers and record-keepers of the Islamic civilization.

In the end, the connotations of the English words and concepts scholars chose to translate Ibn Khaldun's text was too

[6] The phase *mā malakat aymānukum* appears in seven Qur'ānic verses, including, 4:3, 4:24, 4:25, 4:36, 24:33, 24:58, 30:28. While these references are cited to situate ownership of something or someone, Ibn Khaldun sees the explicit reference to 'hand' or 'right hands') as s signal to the work as legitimizing to claims of ownership.

significant and critical to simply dismiss them as disagreements over word choice. Another reason, corollary to the first reason, is this: If a translation is substantively and significantly different from Rosenthal's, and if it is clear that the act of translation is in fact interpretation—rather than unbiased and mechanical rendering of ideas in two different languages—then secondary works based on translations from primary sources should not be treated as equivalent to their corresponding primary sources in an academic context.

Analysis of the primary text to highlight Ibn Khaldun's economic philosophy

To present Ibn Khaldun's thought related to economic philosophy, consider a textual analysis of the relevant Arabic text. This may sound simple enough. However, as explained in the sections on translation of, and secondary works on, Ibn Khaldun, there are many factors that influence such engagement with old texts. Compounding those issues are the many editions of the same work, which vary not only by level of editorial details, but also by content. The editorial (*ẓabṭ; tanqīḥ*) details that distinguish editions include full vocalization of the Arabic text as well as notes (or lack thereof) on the sources the author relied on. The substantive issue is the presence of words and sentences in one edition and their absence in another edition. A translator or reader of any work based on primary sources in the original language must address these factors. One explanation for the substantive variance between editions might be the fact that Ibn Khaldun first drafted *al-Muqaddima* while residing in Algeria, then he produced revised drafts later after his travels east. At least six manuscripts (housed in Turkey and Egypt) have been the basis of translations of parts or all of his *Muqaddima.* The evidence points to Ibn Khaldun having made changes to *al-Muqaddima* even when he lived in Syria, and as late as three years before his death. This explanation for *al-Muqaddima*'s textual variance aligns with the variance in current book editions; North African editions (produced in Morocco, Algerian and Tunisia) often contain words and passages absent from editions produced in Egypt, Syria, or Lebanon.

The most significant variance, however, concerns vocalization—Arabic short vowels (*ḥarakāt*) added to the skeletal text. Because none of Ibn Khaldun's manuscripts were fully vocalized, and to add value to published books of the work, some publishers rely on linguistic experts to fully vocalize the text and add footnotes and marginal notes to explain any ambiguity, highlight historical events for context purposes, or fix spelling errors. It should be noted that adding the vowels to an Arabic skeletal text is a complex and consequential intervention because it is the vowels that fix the meaning of words, assign syntactical and grammatical functions, and provide meaning to sentences. Doing this kind of work requires skill not only in linguistics, but also expertise in cultural idioms, historical context, and content-specific knowledge (topics addressed by the original author, in this case, a very broad list including chemistry, biology, astronomy, arts, engineering, medicine, etc.). In many ways, vocalizing an Arabic text is similar in function and approach to translating an original text.

For the above two reasons, this work relies on a textual analysis of many available editions of the original text. The approach here is both textual and analytical. It is textual in that it parses the Arabic language to find the meaning of words and translate them into English. It is analytical in that it considers context beyond single words, in order to identify the more likely meaning of sentences and paragraphs. To accomplish these steps, this author relied on different editions, including but not limited to editions containing vocalized texts, even as such vocalized texts limit the range of meaning Ibn Khaldun might have had in mind because vowels fix meaning at the level of words. Consulting unvocalized texts that relied on different manuscripts adds greater context and allows for a fresh, holistic look at the original text. Detailed footnotes indicate which edition is used for every citation or direct reference to Ibn Khaldun's ideas. One might see such a method as creating room for an interpreter's bias. To this critique: An interpreter's bias is present in any interpretive work, be it translation or commentary. Some of the more meaningful ways to control for unsupported bias or mitigate for the effects of bias are full transparency with the sources, consideration of a broader range of available sources, reliance on historical and factual context, and engagement with other interpreters from different disciplinary backgrounds and ranges of expertise.

Ibn Khaldun's work is both descriptive and prescriptive. For the descriptive portion, Ibn Khaldun seems to have relied on ethnographic observations, archival research, and archeological artifacts. His prescriptive contribution is driven by deductive and inductive reasoning, data analysis, and the application of Qur'ānic principles as critical instruments of thought and behavior. Taken as a whole, Ibn Khaldun produced a remarkable work of scholarship that is difficult to decipher, insightful in its explanation of events and objects, comprehensive in its coverage, and deeply informative in its record-keeping. Ibn Khaldun was not a passive reporter on, and recorder of, historical events. He was a keen observer of consequential social change, a theoretician deeply interested in identifying the systems that govern the trajectory of development of isolated societies, and a systems thinker who appreciated the interconnectedness of the world. Ibn Khaldun reflected on events based on outcomes—outcomes rooted in lived experiences, which are subject to both the conceptual and practical systems that govern their existence. Understanding Ibn Khaldun's economic philosophy cannot be fully achieved without understanding Ibn Khaldun's conceptualization of civilization and the nature and evolutions of other systems that give rise to human civilizations (Bakar 2017, p.311-33). He addressed these issues in section (*faṣl*) 17 (Ibn Khaldun 2004, p.2:43), which precedes the section on economic activities (*ma`āsh*) (Ibn Khaldun 2004, p.2:65).

As the title of the section of *al-Muqaddima* asserts, civilization[7] is the creation of the State[8] and the existence and persistence of civilization is directly connected to the State and to the persistence and longevity of the State (Ibn Khaldun 2004, p.2:43, 2:47, 2:50-53). As such, civilization becomes a universal social condition that emerges out of enduring urbanization.[9] Civilization is a stage in human societal development that describes a universal system, not a cultural or communal closed system.

Before going further in our analysis, it should be noted that these terms are highly technical. Ibn Khaldun deliberately selected and coined these specific words to denote distinct concepts, ideas, and systems.[10] Additionally, it is critically important to factor in

---

[7] *al-ḥaḍāra.*
[8] *al-dawla.*
[9] *al-`umrān.*
[10] Because Ibn Khaldun is deliberate in his choice of technical terms, and because he coins words that have multiple meanings and implications, some words ought not be translated but instead remain as Arabic words, notwithstanding potential for breaking the reading flow when foreign words are truncated within the text of the narrative. This decision became more appealing when I examined other translations and noticed that the word choice for the translation of certain words was either influenced by personal bias or by the failure to find an English word that is as encompassing and inclusive as the original Arabic. The words

the influence of Berber languages and North African dialects on the writing style and discourse Ibn Khaldun adopted.

First, Ibn Khaldun was the first to coin the words *ḥaḍāra* and *`umrān* in reference to two conditions or states of human development. *`Umrān* is a concept derived from the Arabic word that means, among other things: age, lifecycle, endurance, persistence, and longevity. Ibn Khaldun uses the word *`umrān* to refer to groups of human beings settling and occupying a specific space for a continuous period of time. In other words, it is a reference to people living in clusters, for instance large cities, year-round and for multiple generations, that is to say: enduring urban living. Ibn Khaldun qualifies urbanization this way to distinguish it from regions settled by communities who move around depending on the seasons, other natural patterns, and the availability of natural resources. The uninterrupted, persistent living in the same location is carefully signaled by the choice of the Arabic root, *`-m-r*, which suggests the existence of a living being with a natural lifespan (*`umr*). This qualification of urbanization as a living, time-bound being becomes useful when Ibn Khaldun proposes his theory of the lifespan of dynasties or political regimes tethered to specific human societies.

Ibn Khaldun holds that the existence of *`umrān* is a prerequisite for the emergence of *ḥaḍāra.* In this sense, and contrary to what some Orientalist scholars have suggested, Ibn Khaldun does not think that *`umrān* and *ḥaḍāra* are the same thing. He is explicit in his proposition that, without settled, enduring, populated cities (*`umrān*), there can be no civilization (*ḥaḍāra*). Moreover, the rise of a civilization is dependent on the degree of urbanization, to the extent that there exists a threshold that a settled urban area must attain for a civilization to be born. Yet, the variation among human civilizations is limited only by the level of urbanization, which in turn spurs the intense economic activity and production of goods and services.

Lastly, a third determinant system must be present to enable the emergence of a civilization: the State.[11] The State, according to Ibn Khaldun, is a necessary but not sufficient exclusive factor that must be present for a human civilization to exist and thrive.

ṣinā`a and *murū'a*, for instance, are good examples of the inefficiency and inappropriateness of the words craft and manliness, which were used by other interpreters and translators, including Rosenthal.

[11] *al-dawla.*

The State must exist because it is the force that can secure, redistribute, and grow wealth (*amwāl*). Here, too, Ibn Khaldun distinguishes between a political power holder, like an individual king or a clan, and the political governing institution. In the paradigm Ibn Khaldun proposes, the triad that makes human civilization possible consists of these elements: enduring urban centers, a diversified workforce, and a powerful State. He summarizes this paradigm this way: 'Power and State produce the market of the world' (Ibn Khaldun 2005, p.1:223).[12]

The system that we can envision here, based on Ibn Khaldun's conceptual framework, is one in which *work* becomes the only store of value, represented by the temporal intensity (time) and level of diversification and sophistication of work (skill; expertise). The stability and endurance of urbanization depend on the ability of the State to secure the space (market) within which, and the instruments (currency) with which goods and services are produced and traded. Here, the significance of the idea that work, not money, is the only store of value cannot be overstated. The implication of this view is that work becomes a unit, a metric for measuring the value of goods and services, not price in terms of money.

Ibn Khaldun was not satisfied with simply identifying the three elements that connect the social systems that produce human civilization. He went further to suggest that zeal[13] fulfils its mission when individuals obtain political power, and that rural living evolves to create the conditions that would enable a civilization to thrive (Ibn Khaldun 2005, p.1:226).[14] Therefore, the same way the individual human being goes through a determinate lifecycle that peaks at forty years, each human civilization, too, has a lifecycle (Ibn Khaldun 2004, p.2:55). What he seems to suggest by this analysis is that set goals, be they set by nature or by culture, predetermine the span of the lifecycle of human existence, be it the biological individual, the person, or the social being, the civilization. As a general rule, he suggests that once a being attains their ultimate goal, they predetermine for themselves the span of their lifecycle, its peak, and its phase of decline. Human civilization is the ultimate goal beyond which there is no other goal (Ibn Khaldun 2005,

[12] *'al-sultān wa-'l-dawla sūq al-`ālam.'*
[13] *`aṣabiyya.*
[14] *'al-ḥaḍāra ghāya li-l-badāwa.'*

p.1:226).[15] Therefore, civilization marks the peak of the trajectory of the collective human lifecycle.

What Ibn Khaldun is suggesting here is this: Human beings,[16] individually and collectively, are outcomes of a network of self-regulating systems. Once they subject themselves to the forces of the various systems that power their individual and collective selves to achieve their respective goal (*ghāya*), they are bound to become outcomes, in and of themselves, of the systems they design and deploy to govern their lifestyles.

The connection between the collective and the individual, as Ibn Khaldun sees it, is remarkable. Since the prerequisites of attaining civilizational status are diversified work in a highly competitive environment of settled and enduring urban centers (Ibn Khaldun 2005, p.2:227),[17] the virtues of each activity must be imprinted on the individual human being involved in that specific activity, rendering him an obedient object of the various systems that govern his behavior. Ibn Khaldun ends up tethering human behavior, which is deeply shaped by one's activities for making a living, to human conscience.

With the connections that Ibn Khaldun makes between urbanization, diversified work, and human temperament,[18] he allows us, his readers, to move freely between the moral and the social, between the social and the psychological, and between the material and the emotional forms of existence, showing both interconnectedness and individuality. In other words, we can bypass the idea of whether humans are intrinsically anything—good, bad, courageous, brave, etc.—in favor of understanding that each human being, at their core, is the outcome of their social and environmental systems. Ibn Khaldun unpacks this fluid transition between the social, the psychological, and the moral in human beings in more detail in the section on economic life.

Another important idea that provides more critical context for Ibn Khaldun's theory on civilization is his assertion that the evolution of a human culture to attain the status of a civilization does not represent a virtuous evolution whereby humans attain

---

[15] *ghāya lā mazīd warā'ahā'.*

[16] *al-insān.*

[17] *matā kāna al-`umrānu akthar, kānati al-ḥaḍāratu akmal.*

[18] Keep in mind that Ibn Khaldun held that what humans do, as work, imprints certain traits, ethics, and habits on their soul (*tatalawwanu al-nafsu min tilka al-`awā'id bi-alwānin kathīra*).

moral good through the way they conduct their individual and collective life. For, although he theorizes that intense urbanization necessarily leads to a more complete civilization (Ibn Khaldun 2005, 2:227),[19] he nonetheless cautions that the completeness of a civilization is often accompanied by increased power in the hands of the State. And because powerful states tend to impose higher taxes to meet increased expenditures, the increased taxation leads to increased prices of goods and services, which leads to inflation. This course of events is often irreversible according to Ibn Khaldun, because in enduring, settled urban settings, human beings become bound by the systems—cultural and societal, conceptual and practical—that they designed and by which they live,[20] rendering them incapable of altering their behaviors, including their spending behavior. As such, civilization is always marked by excess.[21] Excess, in the view of Ibn Khaldun, compromises the integrity[22] of the overall system that sustains humans as individuals and as a collective. With disintegration, corruption, exploitation, and dislocation overtaking human values and directing behavior, civilization, in the opinion of Ibn Khaldun, emerges as an immoral, non-virtuous stage of the life of the collective.

> The goal of urbanization (*al-`umrān*) is civilization (*al-ḥaḍāra*); excess (*ṭaraf*) is a likely outcome of civilization; when urbanization achieves its goal—building a civilization, urbanization turns into corruption (*fasād*)... indeed, the ethic gained from civilization through the pursuit of excess is exactly corruption (*`ayn al-fasād*) for the human being is a human being (*insān*) if and only if he is able to balance securing that which benefits him and repelling that which harms him while maintaining upright ethics (*istiqāmati khuluqih*). (Ibn Khaldun 2005, p.2:229)

It should be clear by now why understanding the meaning and functions of civilization, urbanization, and political power, as Ibn

---

[19] *matā kāna al-`umrānu akthar, kānati al-ḥaḍāratu akmal.*[19]

[19] *la yajidūna walijatan `an ḏālika limā malakahum min asri al-`awā'idi wa-ṭā`atiha.'*

[20] *la yajidūna walijatan `an ḏālika limā malakahum min asri al-`awā'idi wa-ṭā`atiha.'*

[21] *taraf.*

[22] *Fasād* is the concept Ibn Khaldun uses to connect corruption of any system when it is deployed in a way or for a purpose it was not intended for.

[22] In the Moroccan edition, the *ma'āsh* section can be found here: Ibn Khaldun (2005), *al-Muqaddima*, Morocco: Khizanat Ibn Khaldun--Bayt al-funun wa-l-`ulum wa-l-adab, 2:243.

Khaldun imagines them, is essential for understanding the economic life of humans regardless of the environment in which they conduct their productive and consumptive activities—be it an urban setting, the precursor to civilizational rise, or in a rural setting, the precursor to urbanization. With these ideas in mind, we shall now focus on several key ideas derived from *al-Muqaddima*'s section on economics and economic life.

Although Ibn Khaldun discusses, in fewer details, themes that are connected to economic life throughout the various sections and chapters of *al-Muqaddima*, it is in Chapter 1 of Book 5 that he focuses specifically on economic topics including subsistence, building wealth, work, investment, capital, types of work, and related subjects. The highlights of his key ideas, therefore, come from this particular section of Ibn Khaldun's *Muqaddima* (Ibn Khaldun 2005, p.2:243).[23]

Ibn Khaldun lays out the framework within which his analysis of economics takes place. He generalizes that God created all that is on Earth and made it available to all human beings, who are the collective beneficiaries. However, when something is obtained (*ḥaṣala; ḥuṣūl*) by the hand (*yad*)[24] of one person, it becomes prohibited for another person to possess it except through exchange for something of close value (*`iwaḍ*). From this framework, key features of Islamic economic theories, as Muslim scholars including Ibn Khaldun promulgate, emerge to the foreground.

First, according to Ibn Khaldun, all that is on Earth is made by an external force, God. All that is made by the external force is a communal[25] resource for all people. Individual human beings may possess[26] some of these otherwise communal resources through work (*`amal*). Once a person gains possession of something through work, it becomes proscribed for someone else to claim it except through an exchange. This exchange could include an instrument that serves as a store of value (*dhakhīra, qinya*), such as gold and

---

[23] In the Moroccan edition, the *ma'āsh* section can be found here: Ibn Khaldun (2005), *al-Muqaddima*, Morocco: Khizanat Ibn Khaldun--Bayt al-funun wa-l-`ulum wa-l-adab, 2:243.
[24] The use of the word *yad* (hand) should not be overlooked or downplayed as a rhetorical, figurative, or linguistic instrument. Given the presence of the same term in the Quranic text, which informed the development of Islamic law, *yad* must mean more than ownership. It must mean, among other things, as Ibn Khaldun suggests, ownership through a particular activity, work, in which a person must utilize their hands for the *ḥuṣūl* to be realized, not any other instrument of acquiring property.
[25] It is communal as signaled by his use of the word *mushtaraka*.
[26] The conceptual transfer of ownership is called *ḥuṣūl*.

silver, which are also created or provided by an external force—God. In Ibn Khaldun's paradigm, these are foundational elements that inform economic life.

Second, since all these elements are internally shared resources that an external force (God) has provided, the only individual element that can be claimed by every person as intrinsically their own, and that can determine a person's social and economic weight, is *work*. As such, according to Ibn Khaldun, all systems of assessment and measurement of economic input and output must use work as their foundational unit—for nothing has a value without work. Aware of this extraordinary generalization, Ibn Khaldun explains that some work is obvious, especially among artisans and craftspersons. But even things of value whose existence may not immediately appear to be the outcome of human work, are in fact so; they are just not as obvious to the casual observer.

For this definition of work to hold, Ibn Khaldun distinguishes between two outcomes of work. Subsistence (*rizq*) is any outcome of work that results in providing human beings with necessities including food, clothing, shelter, and other goods and services that sustain and preserve the well-being of the human being. Ibn Khaldun argues that on the surface, securing (*ḥuṣūl*) some of these basic needs, like food from plants that grow due to natural processes like rain and sunlight, may not require work. In reality, he adds, such natural interventions go in tandem with human labor (*mu`īn*), for a person must still exert some effort, or work, to process the product and consume it. Securing *rizq* (*taḥṣīl al-rizq*) can occur through a number of systems: fishing and hunting (*iṣṭiyād*), taxation-based income that the State provides (*jibāya*), domestication (*tadjīn*) of animals, or cultivation of plants (*falaḥan*).

The second outcome of work is earnings, income, or earned income (*kasb*). *Kasb*, for him, is all that is acquired (*mutamallak*) through one's work and one's power (*sa`y*, *qudra*) and that is above and beyond one's *rizq*. *Kasb* can be achieved through direct[27] human work, through crafting and skilled labor (*ṣanā`i*), or through trade (*tijāra*). Ibn Khaldun does not see any other legitimate paths for subsistence or for earned income.

[27] Ibn Khaldun explicitly states that *kasb* is through (direct) human work, which can be contrasted to indirect human work in which humans exploit animals or other human beings to do work for them.

It is a mistake to assume that Ibn Khaldun thought that *rizq* (subsistence) can be derived only from some basic activities like hunting, fishing, and farming. The inclusion of taxation as a source for subsistence connects subsistence to all other activities that result in *kasb* (earned income). Since the State often acts through levying taxes and fees on all economic activities to predetermine the political economy of the nation, Ibn Khaldun envisions *rizq* to be a base income that every human being must secure regardless of their ability or disability, regardless of their skill, and regardless of their access to capital. If a person is able to work, they will be able to provide subsistence for themselves and for those under their care. If they are unable to work, then it is the responsibility of the State, through taxation, to provide for those who cannot provide subsistence for themselves and for those under their responsibility. In this paradigm, the State is under the obligation to provide that base level of income, *rizq*, and is under the prohibition of not taxing basic income (*rizq*). This distinction is important within the context of modern taxation regimes that tax income, which stands in contrast to Islamic taxation systems that effect wealth but not exclusively income.

This framing of work as a central currency allows Ibn Khaldun to proceed to categorize and catalog the types of work humans perform for both subsistence and for building wealth. In this context, he coins the word *ṣinā`a* (pl. *ṣanā'ï`*) to refer to all activities that would allow one to make a living (*rizq*) or to build wealth (*kasb*). It is in this context, then, that Ibn Khaldun makes the remarkable claim that what a person does for a living will decide what kind of a person, ethically and morally speaking, that person would be or is. Ibn Khaldun holds that without work, humans are unable to access and consume the resources God provides. Therefore, any attempt to generate income without work is necessarily exploitative and leads to harming the integrity of systems (*fasād*) that sustain human beings.

In this section, as is the case in all of his work, Ibn Khaldun combines a remarkable understanding of the professions and activities he describes with a sharp mind that enables him to prescribe provocative and intriguing theories and explanations. A good translation that attempts to match Ibn Khaldun's appreciation of the use of language to inform and intrigue should do his work on economics justice. Here it would suffice to highlight what might be some of his consequential ideas.

His insistence that human beings are the product of what they do should be subject of critical examination for scholars from a number of disciplines today, especially given the dominance of some philosophical and scientific approaches that do not share that point of view.

Another aspect of Ibn Khaldun's thought seemingly absent from modern scholars' critical analyses of his work is his approach as a systems thinker. The idea that all events are outcomes of systems, and that human beings are subject to natural systems as well as to additional systems that they design themselves and apply to their lives, is compelling and deeply original when taken in the context of Islamic thought and beyond during that time. His notion that systems imprint their outcomes on their subjects is fascinating for many reasons.

For instance, thinking in terms of systems as understood by Ibn Khaldun would suggest, among other things, that it is not important or useful to think that people are not smart and dumb because they are created so. Rather, it is more constructive, according to Ibn Khaldun, to think that people are smart, dumb, deceitful, hypocritical, courageous, cowardly, noble, meek, humble, or any other characteristic through their *ṣinā`a*. The things human beings do in life over a long period of time require of them certain behavioral traits, and the habits that make them successful in their line of work also imprint on them the traits built from those habits. In other words, what one does for a profession or vocation rewrites one's conscience and sense of self.

What Ibn Khaldun is suggesting, through this connection of all the systems that act on the human being, is that the material world is ultimately connected to the human mind to a degree that the human soul carries the influences of lived experience beyond their material existence. He posits that fragments of human work live in the memory of the collective, with the power to influence the cultures and conditions of future generations. He used the idea of the persistence of lived experience in the form of a spiritual 'haunting' power when he explained the consequences of exploitative trade practices that manipulate peoples' access to basic needs.

Also of significance is Ibn Khaldun's vision of the State as an institution and a determinant system that has the power, and often the will, to override market-based systems and rules, to promote one form of trade over another (*al-dawla hiya al-sūq al-a'ẓam*)

(Ibn Khaldun 2004, p.2:95). Specifically, he held that the State is the determinant system when it comes to creating and sustaining crafts because it can create demand. It can fund the learning and transfer of crafts, and it can fund the markets for the products of such crafts. If the State wishes to terminate or devalue a craft and its product it can do so, even if demand is there. Markets alone cannot create demand unless the State wills it. This stream of thought is not only intriguing in its own historical and cultural contexts, but also relevant given the competing visions in the modern area of political economy.

Summarizing Ibn Khaldun's most significant contributions

After analyzing Ibn Khaldun's economic philosophy, this author wishes to highlight a few ideas that stand out and that might be deserving of further inquiry.

One idea can be characterized as Ibn Khaldun's theory on the economic origins of human conscience. It is derived from the notion that a human being's values, morals, ethics, and temperaments are outcomes of what they regularly do to make a living (*ma'āsh*). Ibn Khaldun signals this proposition more clearly when he argues that some professions (*ṣanā'i*) do imprint certain traits and moral principles on their holders. For instance, Ibn Khaldun contends that the ethics and morality of traders or merchants is 'below the ethics and morality of nobles and kings,' for the profession confers certain traits on those who undertake it' (Ibn Khaldun 2004, p.2:75, 2:89).

While discussing monopoly (*iḥtikār*), Ibn Khaldun asserts the notion of human souls being attached to their basic needs (food, shelter, clothes) to the extent that if a merchant or a tax collector leverages their control over the basic needs of persons, through monopoly or levies, the collective souls of these persons who were denied access to basic needs or whose basic needs were exploited to enrich the merchant or the tax collector will haunt these merchants, resulting in the disappearance and loss of their profit (*talaf wa-khusrān al-fā'ida*) or the corruption of their wealth (Ibn Khaldun 2004, p.2:87).[28] Ibn Khaldun asserts that what a person does in life and the duration of their connection to their profession has an effect on their conscience: 'Good deeds have virtuous effects and bad actions return non-virtuous effects, and the moral effects would

[28] *Fasād al-ribḥ*.

endure if they take hold early and repeat' (Ibn Khaldun 2004, p.2:89).[29] He explains that merchants who associate with other merchants will acquire the worst traits, for the imprinting of merchants' ethics is accretive and proportional to the frequency of contact a merchant has with those in the same or related profession (Ibn Khaldun 2004, p.2:89).[30] Ibn Khaldun further asserts that ability, acquired or otherwise, colors the conscience of the person and limits its ability to acquire a second *ṣināʿa* (Ibn Khaldun 2004, p.2:100).[31]

Although Ibn Khaldun makes the case for connecting a human's conscience to what they do in life by referencing merchants and traders as the best candidates for the power of the profession to imprint certain values in the human conscience, there are enough references in *al-Muqaddima* alone that suggest that he would generalize this kind of effect across any profession. The difference is that he sees different professions imprinting different values onto their holders. Interestingly, he also connects the professions that imprint the least virtuous traits to happiness (*sa`āda*), as in the case of being submissive or subservient and cajoling (*al-khuḍū' wa-l-tamalluq*); the same traits are also paths for acquiring prestige (*jāh*) and prestige is the path to acquiring happiness (*sa'āda*) and earnings (*kasb*). He concludes that cajoling produces the most people with wealth (*tharwa*) and happiness (Ibn Khaldun 2004, p.2:78).

This connection is fascinating considering that Ibn Khaldun is a systems thinker who connects what appear to be unrelated, 'unconnectable' systems, like financial transactions and human souls and consciences. The reason Ibn Khaldun's propositions and his framework of analysis needs more attention is that he insists on work being the central engine that produces outcomes. Without work, no events can be achieved. At the same time, he connects humans' consciences to the work in which they engage.

Another significant proposition is Ibn Khaldun's contention that work is the basis of value and values. He insists that work should be the basis of determining value, not the arbitrary assignment of price or even the price determined by the market. This is significant, because when read in a comparative context, it suggests

[29] *Tarsukh 'in sabaqat wa-takarrarat.*
[30] *Kānat radā'atu tilka al-khuliqi `indahu ashadd.*
[31] *al-malakāt sifatu al-nafsi wa-alwāni fa-lā tazdaḥimu mujtami`atan.*

that the valuation of any object or event must be based on the work performed to achieve its realization. In other words, Ibn Khaldun might be suggesting the use of work as a metric of valuation not only for trade purposes, but for assessment as well. With this in mind, informing Ibn Khaldun's worldview is his proposition that work is central and universal, and because it is central and universal it shapes the human conscience, and because it shapes the human conscience, there must be some judgements about which lines of work or paths for making a living are legitimate and which are not. His list of *ṣanā'i`* contains explicit and implicit judgments about each one, with trade being less favored perhaps because of the high risk of monopolistic practices associated with it or perhaps because traders do not actually produce goods and services, but merely sell them and make a profit from the price fluctuation (Ibn Khaldun 2004, p.2:68).

By connecting trade (*tijāra*) as the activity that produces income (*kasb*) through the packaging and distribution of goods and services produced by people who have *ṣanā'i`*, and that people with *ṣanā'i`* flourish in urban settings, and that urban settings are a prerequisite for the rise of human civilizations, one can easily see the holistic approach, the systems thinking framework through which Ibn Khaldun sees the world—the universe—when one pays attention to his religious references.

The impact and implication of Ibn Khaldun's ideas globally are unmistakable. First, he concluded that the surest paths to profit through trade involves the sale of goods and services in local markets when local market conditions change, which can be triggered by hoarding (a form of *iḥtikār*) or transporting local goods to distant countries where prices are higher (Ibn Khaldun 2004, p.2:83, 2:86). Second, he determined *iḥtikār* to be risky for social and religious reasons. The more attractive path, in this scenario, is cross-border trade, which helps merchants who wish to avoid *iḥtikār* make significant profit. Historically, this explains the appeal of cross-border trading to Muslim merchants, who ended up reviving and enriching the ancient Silk Road. Socially, one must imagine the impact of cross-border trade on indigenous economies related to issues of equity, autonomy, sustainability and access and use of resources. Ibn Khaldun's ideas have local and global impact and implications.

In addition to the suggested connection between the kind of work and the kind of a human being that would emerge out of doing a certain kind of work, this article proposes that Ibn Khaldun's philosophy cannot be characterized as coherent without finding that he relied on a systems thinking approach that defines a system as a divisible whole in terms of structure, and indivisible unity in terms of function. That is, to think of the existence of events as isolated systems with specific purposes that are organically connected to each other through physical and conceptual links. For example, a universal event, such as the decline of a human civilization, can be traced back to the values systems that individual human beings subscribe to and act upon, which can be traced to work, the kind of work the individual would regularly perform.

The complexity of these claims makes it necessary to introduce them here for the purpose of recommending future research endeavors, as they cannot be accommodated in this work since it is limited by structure, medium, and convention. The economic origin of human conscience is a compelling stream of thought that should be pursued in a standalone work for it is, in the view of this author, the most fascinating and intriguing idea that can be derived from Ibn Khaldun's work on economic activities and economic systems—the alleged impact of one's profession on their ethics and morality.

Concluding thoughts

As a systems thinker, Ibn Khaldun believed deeply that knowledge is an accretive, accumulated body of information. In this way he differs from modern scholars, for whom originality of thought is more valuable—even an obsessive priority—over accumulated knowledge. Ibn Khaldun was well aware that the knowledge he acquired was the providence of generations of scholars and thinkers that preceded him. As a product of modern scholars, perhaps responding to modern scholarship, this author may have indirectly emphasized the fact that Ibn Khaldun was an original thinker more than Ibn Khaldun would have cared to think of himself. Perhaps our modern boilerplate scientific method that requires a literature review section before producing our own analysis is what compels us to theorize and comment on earlier scholars' original thought. It should not be the point of discussion here. What should be promoted is for modern scholars to examine Ibn Khaldun's contributions on the basis of their own merit and as presented in their original language.

This introductory essay is not intended to be a substitute for direct engagement with Ibn Khaldun's thought in translation or in its original language. It is intended to encourage other researchers and scholars from other disciplines to take a fresh look at Ibn Khaldun's work in its own context and with open minds—minds as free as possible from the limitations of our cultural and professional biases. Such renewed attention would require us to consider the fact that it is difficult, but possible, to see and access that which our 'work' allows us to read and think, and that we are, after all, the products of the systems that govern our *ṣinā`a*—one of Ibn Khaldun's theories that connects our material world to our conscience.

Ahmed E. Souaiaia, University of Iowa, Iowa City, IA, USA.

September 8, 2023.

References

Bakar, Osman (2017), 'Towards A New Science of Civilization. A Synthetic Study of the Philosophical Views of al-Farabi, Ibn Khaldun, Arnold Toynbee, and Samuel Huntington', *Synthesis Philosophica* 31 (2), 311-333.

Boulakia, Jean David C. (1971), 'Ibn Khaldûn: A Fourteenth-Century Economist', *Journal of Political Economy*, 79 (5), 1105–1118.

Dale, Stephen Frederic (2006), 'Ibn Khaldun: The Last Greek and the First Annaliste Historian', *International Journal of Middle East Studies*, 38 (3) 431–451.

de Muijnck, Sam, and Joris Tieleman (2021), 'Building Block 4: History of Economic Thought & Methods', in *Economy Studies: A Guide to Rethinking Economics Education,* Amsterdam University Press, pp. 187–99.

Gellner, Ernest (1975), 'Cohesion and Identity: The Maghreb from Ibn Khaldun to Emile Durkheim', *Government and Opposition*, 10 (2), 203–18.

Gibb, H. A. R. (1933), 'The Islamic Background of Ibn Khaldun's Political Theory', *Bulletin of the School of Oriental Studies*, 7 (1), 23–31.

Ibn Khaldun (1958), *The Muqaddimah: An Introduction to History,* English edition, Franz Rosenthal (translator), Pantheon Books.

Ibn Khaldun (1969), *Al Muqaddimah*, Franz Rosenthal (translator), Bollingen Series XLIII. Accessed at https://archive.org/details/al-muqaddimah-by-ibn-khaldun-and-translated-by-franz-rosenthal/mode/2up

Ibn Khaldun (2001), *Muqaddimat Ibn Khaldun,* Harat Hrik: Dar al-Fikr li-tiba`a wa-l-nashr wa-l-tawzi`, Beirut, Lebanon.

Ibn Khaldun (2004), *Muqaddimat Ibn Khaldun*, Damascus: Dar Ya`rab.

Ibn Khaldun (2005), *al-Muqaddima*, Morocco: Khizanat Ibn Khaldun--Bayt al-funun wa-l-`ulum wa-l-adab.

Ibn Khaldun (2007), *Kitab al-`ibar wa-diwan al-mubtada' wa-l-khabar fi tarikh al-`arab wa-l-barbar waman `asarahum min thawi al-sha'n al-akbar*, Tunis: al-Qayrawan li-l-nashr.

Ibn Khaldun (2007), *Muqaddimat Ibn Khaldun*, Cairo: Dar al-sha`b,

Ibn Khaldun, *Diwan al-mubtada' wa-l-khabar fi tarikh al-`arab wa-l-barbar waman `asarahum min thawi al-sha'n al-akbar, Muqaddimat.*

Rosen, Lawrence (2005), 'Theorizing from within: Ibn Khaldun and His Political Culture', *Contemporary Sociology*, 34 (6), 596–599.

Spengler, J. J. (1964), 'Economic Thought of Islam: Ibn Khaldun', *Comparative Studies in Society and History*, 6 (3), 268–306.

Muqaddima of Ibn Khaldun, Book One, Chapter Five: Making a Living

1. On the Origins and Meaning of Subsistence and Earnings

> In this chapter, we explore the ways people make a living (*ma`āsh*), including earnings (*kasb*) and skills and occupations useful for making a living (*ṣanā'i`*); and define and explain subsistence (*rizq*) and earnings, with earnings being the true value of all human activities.

Know that the human being, by nature, lacks (*muftaqir*) all that which enables them to be strong and develop under all circumstances and during all phases of their growth: from birth to when they attain full strength to when they reach old age. "God is the Rich and you people are the Poor." And it is God Almighty who created all that is in the world for the benefit of the human being and He reminded them of it in many verses of His Book wherein He says: "He created for you all that which is in the heavens and all that which is on Earth; all of it, from Him to you."[32] He empowered you over the sea, He empowered you over space, and He empowered you over animal and beast. Much other evidence points to His providence.

The power and reach of humankind over the world and over what is in the world is incidental to being God's regent on Earth. The power of each and every member of humankind is spread in partnership among all human beings in such regency. That which is claimed by one human being becomes proscribed on another unless exchanged. For when a human being becomes self-sufficiently

[32] Qur'an: *al-Jathiyah*, 13.

able and surpasses the phase of weakness, he would strive to acquire earnings (*makāsib*) in order to spend what God has given him from them in securing his needs and necessities by paying the cost of exchanging it. God Almighty says: "Seek subsistence (*rizq*) at God," which may be accomplished without effort on his part, such as the case of subsistence (*rizq*) derived from farming when he would benefit from rain and the like. However, the rain is only contributory, for he must add his own effort to it for the earnings (*makāsib*) to belong to him and become earned living income (*ma`āshan*). When such earnings (*makāsib*) cover only necessities and basic needs, it is called making a living (*ma`āsh*); and when such earnings exceed the cost of necessities and basic needs, then it is called wealth and riches (*riyash, mutamail*). Moreover, when that which is obtained or acquired, if he benefits from its returns and its fruits are obtained from spending on his welfare and needs, it shall be called subsistence (*rizq*).

The Prophet, may God's prayers and peace be upon him (*ṣalla allāhu alayhi wa-sallam*), said: "Belong to you (human being) from your wealth that which you ate to consumption, or wore until it is worn out, or you gave in charity and was consummated." If something was not used to meet the immediate needs and wellbeing, then it shall not be called subsistence (*rizq*) for the owner; the owned surplus, then, when acquired through the owner's work and efforts, shall be called earned income or earnings (*kasb*).

For example, inherited legacy, for the deceased (*hālik*), is called earnings—and it cannot be called subsistence (*rizq*), for the deceased is not benefiting from it. However, when the heirs consume it and benefit from it, then it will be called subsistence (*rizq*).

This is the definition of what is called subsistence (*rizq*) according to the Sunnis. The Mu`tazila, however, stipulated that it can be called subsistence (*rizq*) if and only if it can be owned; for them that which cannot be owned[33] cannot be called subsistence (*rizq*). Therefore, they excluded usurped property and things that

[33] *lā yaṣuḥ tamallukuh.*

are proscribed (*ḥarām*); such things cannot be called subsistence (*rizq*). The Mu`tazila scholars contend that God almighty provides (*yarziq*) the usurper, the aggressor; the believer, and the non-believer; for He is merciful, and His guidance reaches whomever He wills. They provide numerous arguments for this, but this is not the place to explain them. However, know that earned income (*kasb*) is pursued through labor and realized through acquisition. As for subsistence, it must result from striving and work, even using or seeking. God says: "Seek subsistence at God," for even the power to exert the effort to obtain subsistence is ultimately God's determination, inspiration, and providence. Everything is from God. Therefore, human work is necessary for every earned and/or accrued wealth. For when the income is a result of work, such as, for example, being the outcome of skilled expertise, then it is obvious. However, if the income is acquired from animals, plants, or minerals, it must be resulting, in part, from human work, as one can see. Otherwise, no income could be acquired, and no benefit can be derived therefrom.

Moreover, God almighty created the two mineral stones, gold and silver, as store of value for any kind of wealth; the two are, most likely, the reserve and store of value for all peoples of the world. Even if, sometimes, things other than gold and silver are acquired in their stead, it is only for the purpose of acquiring the two for the purpose of using their as substitute depending on the conditions of the markets where they are not adopted. Therefore, these two (gold and silver) are at the origin of earnings (*makāsib*), added value (*qinya*), and reserve (*dhakhīra*) of wealth.

With all this is established, know, then, that that which the human being improves on or acquires in the form of wealth, when resulting from artisan enterprise, then, added-value from it is the value realized from his labor, which is what is meant by added-value (*qinya*); work cannot be meant by added-value (*qinya*). It may be the case that work is also present in some other enterprises, such as trade (*tijāra*) and tailoring (*ḥiyāka*), which include wood and cloth. However, work in such artisan enterprises is more[34], which makes its value more as well, even if it were not the outcome of artisan activities, for there must be a value (*qīma*) in that benefit (*mafād*). With that said, the added-value is the factoring in of the value of work that produced it, for if it were not for work, it would not have an added-value.

Work can be easily observed in the artisan enterprise, which makes assigning a value to work easy and obvious, be it a small or large value. In other cases, work may be hidden and hard to observe as is the case with the prices of foodstuffs. In this case, the work and expenditures invested in them can be observed in the prices of grains; as we have stated before, these costs are hidden in regions where farming requires less effort that only few observers will be able to notice.

Therefore, it is clear that profits (*manāfa`*) and earnings (*muktasabāt*), all of them or for most of them, are values of work undertaken by humans. That which we call subsistence (*rizq*) is what is used for immediate benefit. The meaning of earnings (*kasb*) and subsistence (*rizq*) shall be clear by now; the meaning of both words has been explained.

Know that when work is all or partially gone due to a decrease in settled urbanization (*`umrān*), God signals the dissipation of earnings. You should be able to observe that cities with few inhabitants have smaller subsistence (*rizq*) and earnings, or none at all, due to shortage in human work (*a`māl*; sing. *`amal*). Whereas for countries (*amṣār*) with large cities and a larger workforce, their inhabitants enjoy more favorable conditions and have more luxuries, as we have stated before.

Based on this, this is commonly said about a country: If its urban cities become sparsely populated, subsistence therein will disappear to the extent that even the flow of springs and rivers stop in waste areas, for springs flow only if they are dug out and when

[34] Work in such artisan enterprises is more work, meaning either time, skill, investment, or energy.

the water is drawn, which require human work analogous to the udders of animals. Springs that are not dug out and from which no water is drawn disappear in the ground completely, the same way udders dry up when they are not milked. This can be observed in countries where springs existed during times of thriving urban centers, then they[35] are ruined, and the water of the springs disappeared completely in the ground, as if it had never existed; and God predetermines the night and the day.

[35] Urban centers.

2. On Ways, Means, and Methods of Making a Living

It should be known that making a living (*ma`āsh*) refers to seeking subsistence and the work to obtain it. The word *ma`āsh* is a place form derived from the word *`aysh* (living, or life). The form of the word *ma`āsh* suggests that, since the word *`aysh* means life or living, is[36] not obtained unless through *`aysh*; thus, the word *ma`āsh* was coined for making a living for emphasis.[37]

As to the acquisition of subsistence and its growth, there are a number of paths to that. Subsistence can be taken away and wrestled away from another person through the power of an established law, and this would be called customs and taxation. Subsistence can also be a wild animal used and killed by targeting it on land or in water, which is called hunting. Or subsistence can be derived from domesticated animals by extracting benefits from them that are customary among people, such as milk from animals, silk from silkworms, and honey from bees. Or it can be from plants of the greeneries and trees through cultivating and preparing them to produce their fruits, and all of this is called agriculture (*falḥ*).

Income can also result from human work applied to specific materials, and it is called *ṣanā'i`*, including writing, trading, tailoring, shoemaking, horsemanship, and their like. Or it may be applied to nonspecific materials, which are all other vocations and undertakings.

Income may result from goods and the preparation thereof for use in barter. Owners of such goods could dominate the domestic market by hoarding these goods and waiting for favorable

[36] The word "it" references *ma'āsh*.

[37] It's important to note here in Ibn Khaldun's explanation that he hones in on being alive as a core component of "making a living," in other words placing emphasis on "living" in the phrase "making a living." He does this to not only say that one needs subsistence in order to go on living, but to underscore the reverse as well: One must be living—that is, alive—in order to reap subsistence. This goes counter to many modern systems, which allow deceased individuals to make money.

conditions to sell them with a profit margin. This activity is called commerce.

These are, then, the different ways and means of making a living, which is the meaning referenced by experts in literature and philosophy including al-Hariri and others, who said: "making a living can come from political leadership (*imāra*), commerce (*tijāra*), agriculture (*filāḥa*), or manufacturing (*ṣināʿa*)."

As for political leadership, it is not a natural way of making a living (*maʿāsh*). Therefore, we will not expand on it here, for we have already discussed it in Section Two of the chapter on royal taxation and the people in charge of it.

As for agriculture (*filāḥa*), manufacturing (*ṣināʿa*), and commerce (*tijāra*), these are natural ways of making a living; where agriculture being the first form, and by its very nature, supersedes the others since it is simple and innately natural, not requiring much theoretical training or scientific learning. For this reason, its origin is attributed to Adam, the father of humankind—the first teacher and custodian of it—signaling that it is the oldest way of making a living and the most suitable to nature.

Manufacturing is the second of the two and comes after agriculture for it is complex and scientific, needing the expenditure of ideas and theories, making it an area mostly exclusive to the people who live in large cities, which[38] ensues from rural living and secondary to it. In this sense, manufacturing was attributed to Idris, the second father of humankind. Inspired by divine revelation, he invented manufacturing for the benefit of humans who would come after him.

Commerce, although a natural way for earning an income, is, nonetheless, due to its practices and its ways, a collection of tricks designed to generate profit from the difference between the buy and sale prices. Therefore, the law permits adjustable pricing (*mukāsaba*) in commerce, since commerce contains a form of

[38] The practice of people living in large cities ensues from rural living and is secondary to rural living.

gambling—different only in that it is not about taking the property of others freely (without reciprocity). Therefore, it is legitimate. And God is a better knower.

3. On How Being a Servant is not a Natural Way of Making a Living

It should be known that the powerholder (Sultan) depends on the services of soldiers, policemen, and secretaries in all the departments of governing (*imāra*) and royal affairs (*mulk*). For each department, the powerholder would rely on one who knows that his riches are connected to servitude of he[39] who would provide for their[40] subsistence from his treasury. All this is included in governance and its payroll since all of them[41] are subject to the rule of governing and grand ownership is the mainstream of their tributaries.

What is below that form of service is made possible by the fact that most of those who live in luxury look down upon taking care of their own personal needs or are unable to do so due their upbringing, which has cultured in them certain attitudes including indulging themselves in enjoying luxury. Consequently, they employ people who will take care of such things for them in return for a cut from their wealth in the form of wages. This arrangement is not praiseworthy when judged from the standard of masculinity (*rujūliyya*), where trusting the securing of one's needs to someone else is equivalent to inability. Additionally, hiring servants adds to the bureaucracy and taxes and indicates inability and lack of masculinity, both of which must be avoided in the school of masculinism[42] (*rujūliyya*). However, habits invert human nature into what is normal, for the human being is the product of their habits not the product of their biological ancestry.

[39] The powerholder
[40] The powerholder's servants
[41] The people the powerholder employs
[42] This is not in reference to the modern ideology of masculinism, which positions itself as an anti-feminist movement seeking greater rights for men; rather, it is referencing the social roles that are part of Islamic societies. These roles are assigned based on age and sex, rather than social hierarchy. In this passage, which clearly pre-dates modern "masculinism" ideology, "masculinism" references that assigned role—and its ensuing expectations of work and ability—that men bear in society.

Nonetheless, the servant who would accomplish the tasks entrusted to them and with whom one's property is safe due to their own wealth is almost nonexistent since a hired servant is one of four types:

1. A servant could be both capable of doing what he was hired for and trustworthy in his handling of the property that is under his care.
2. A servant could be neither capable of doing what he was hired for nor trustworthy in his handling of the property that is under his care.
3. A servant could be not capable of doing what he was hired for but trustworthy in his handling of the property that is under his care.
4. A servant could be capable of doing what he was hired for but not trustworthy in his handling of the property that is under his care.

As to the case where the servant is both a capable and trustworthy servant, no one would in any way be able to secure the employment of such a person, for, with his capability and trustworthiness, he would have no need for persons of lower rank, and he would frown upon accepting the wages offered for his service, because he could get more.[43] Such a person is employed only by princes with high social standing who might have a need for someone who could preserve or augment their social standing, as a general rule.

As to the second case, where the servant is neither capable nor trustworthy, such a person should not be employed by any intelligent person, because he will do damage to his employer on both counts: He will bring losses due to his inaptitude and he will defraud his employer by stealing his property—making such a servant a liability to his employer. These two types—no one wishes to employ them.

We are now left with the employment of the other two kinds of servants: trustworthy but incapable and capable but not

[43] "More" refers to higher wages

trustworthy servants. People are divided into two schools of thought over which they would prefer of the two types. Each of the two preferences has specific context.

The capable but not trustworthy one might be preferred over the other because he would not cause damage due to inaptitude, but one can guard against his treachery as much as one is capable. As to the incapable servant who may cause damage due to his inaptitude, even if such a servant is trustworthy, the damage due to inaptitude is higher than the benefits of their character—being trustworthy. You should know this about the reliance on service providers and consider it a rule when contemplating hire of service providers. And God, almighty, wills all things.

4. On How Seeking Money from Buried Objects and Treasures is not a Natural Way of Making a Living

Know that many weak-minded persons in cities hope to extract wealth from under the ground and wish to make some income from it. They believe that the wealth of the previous communities is stored, all of it, underground and sealed with magic talismans. These seals, they believe, can be broken only by one who stumbles upon the science of such magic and who has obtained the proper incense, prayers, and sacrifices necessary to open them.

The inhabitants of the cities in of *Ifrīqiyya*[44] thought that the foreigners of the pre-Islamic times who lived in the region buried their wealth and memorialized it in written documents that would preserve it until such time when they are able to retrieve it.

The inhabitants of the cities in the east held similar beliefs about the Coptic, Roman (Byzantine), and the Persian civilizations. They shared stories about this that resemble myth, including stories about treasure hunters, who did not know the talisman, or the story connected with it, and who dug where they believed the wealth and money was buried only to find the place empty or inhabited by worms. Other stories claim that some treasure hunters did find the buried wealth, but armed guards stood guard over it. In another story yet, the earth shook as if it were threatening to swallow them and many other foolish stories.

In the west, in *al-Maghrib*, many Berber students who were unable to make a living by natural ways and means, they would approach affluent people with papers with torn margins containing either non-Arab writing or what they claimed to be the translation of a document written by the owner of buried treasures, holding clues to the place. These students would explain that they are seeking the help of the affluent people for two reasons: compensation for finding and digging out the wealth and to secure protection of influential people against trespass charges. Occasionally, one of these treasure hunters displays strange information or some remarkable trick of magic with which he fools people into believing

[44] Mainly modern-day Tunisia and neighboring regions, not to be confused with *Ifrīqiyā*, which refers to the continent of Africa.

his other claims, although, in fact, he knew nothing of magic and (magical) procedures.

Most weak-minded people wish to do their digging with others and to be protected by the darkness of the night while they do it. They were afraid of watchers and government spies. When they did not turn anything up, they would put the blame upon their ignorance of the talisman with which the buried money was sealed. Thus, they deceived themselves as to the failure of their hopes.

In addition to weak-mindedness, a common motive that leads people to hunt for treasure is their inability to make a living through one of the natural ways that lead to earnings, such as commerce, agriculture, or artisanship. Therefore, they try to make a living in devious ways and unnatural ways like treasure hunting and the like. They fail as a result of their inability to strive to earn and as the outcome of their inclination for subsisting without the troubles that come with hard work, hardships and extreme labor that exceeds their shortcut—add to that the fact that they risk punishment for violating the law.

Occasionally, a principal motive leading people to hunt for treasures is the fact that they have become used to ever-increasing, limitless luxury and excessive customs. Consequently, the various ways and means of earnings cannot keep pace with and do not pay for the demands of such lifestyle. Therefore, when such a person fails to earn wealth through natural ways, the only inspiration that strikes them is to hope that there is great wealth that can be claimed in one shot and without any cost. Thus, they become eager to find treasures and they concentrate all their efforts on that goal. Subsequently, most of those who can be observed to be eager to hunt for treasures are people used to living in excess and luxury like people associated with the ruling class and the inhabitants of large urban areas such as Cairo (Egypt) and its like, where we find that many such people are enthralled by the search for such "unclaimed" wealth and eager to claim it for themselves—seeking information about its abnormalities from travelers the same way they would seek information about chemistry.

I was told that the inhabitants of Cairo (Egypt) engage with whomever they encounter among students coming from *al-Maghrib* hoping that, with their help, they may find some buried wealth or treasures. They would further investigate how to divert waterways, for they believed that most of all buried treasures are under the streamways of the Nile and that the Nile is the largest cover of the buried wealth and treasures in those horizons. Persons who possess the aforementioned made-up records further camouflage the treasures because the Nile flows over their locations. Thus, they conceal their lies to make a living. They conceal them from those who hear their claims about the drying or diversion of water through magic to reach their goals. In such regions, magic is passed generation to generation and its effects endure in their lands as their ruins attest to. The story of Pharaoh's magicians testifies to their expertise in that as well.

The people of the Maghrib have preserved a poem they attribute to the wisemen of the East. In it, how to divert water into the ground through magic is prescribed, and the poem is this:

> Seeker of the secret diverting water into the ground, listen to the true words of an expert;
>
> Abandon what they have compiled in their books; it is all falsehoods and deceptive remarks;
>
> That people have written in books, And listen to my truthful word and advice;
>
> Listen to my truthful statement and advice; If you are one of those who do not believe in falsehood;
>
> If you want to divert a well into the ground, and knowing this has escaped all mind;
>
> Pictures like yours that stopped, And the head is that of a young lion in its roundedness shape.
>
> His two hands holding the rope that is, pulling out the bucket from the bottom of a well;
>
> On his breast, an "h" as you have seen it,
>
> Of the number of divorce [3] and be careful of repeat;
>
> And a stroke upon the T's without touching,
>
> Walking like the fearless, clever, and skillful;

Around all, a square-lined, rather than spherical;

Slaughter a bird over it and smear its (blood) upon it, and after the slaughtering, purify it with incense;

With sandarac, frankincense, storax, and costus root and cover it with a silk garment;

It should be red or a yellow, not blue one, no green or dark color in it;

Threads of white wool should hold it together, or purest red colors of red;

The rising should be Leo, which they had already explained, and the start of the month should not moonlight;

And the moon should be connected with the luck of Mercury, on a Saturday be the hour of reckoning.

In my opinion, I think that they meant that the platforms must be between their feet as if he is walking over it; and that this poem is the work of swindlers. These swindlers employ astounding techniques and their claims and lies allow them to take up residence in famous mansions and houses known for this. They dig holes in them making underground cells where they put evidence that they forged and wrote down. They would, then, go to some weak-minded person with these lists. They would urge them to rent the residence and live there. They suggest to them that the building contains a buried treasure of indescribable size. They ask for money to buy potions and incense, in order to solve the talismans. They promise him that they will produce evidence that they themselves had placed there and that were of their own making. He[45] gets excited by the things he sees. He is deceived and taken in by them without knowing it. Meanwhile, the swindlers use among themselves a linguistic terminology with the help of which they inveigle their marks, and keep them in ignorance of what they say concerning the

[45] The weak-minded person and victim of this scam.

digging, incense, slaughtering of animals, and the other such things that they do.

Truth be told about this matter: It is baseless scientifically and historically. It should be noted that treasure, though it might exist, is a rarity and can be found by coincidence, not as the outcome of a deliberate system designed for locating it. Here is the reason: The concealment of treasures was not a deliberate attempt to avoid loss to the extent that people would store their wealth under the ground and seal it with talismans. This has never been the case neither in ancient nor in recent times. The *rikāz* mentioned in the Hadith tradition, and included by *fiqh* scholars in inheritance law, which was buried during the *jāhiliyya* time, even that, is found by accident, not intentionally setting out to find it. Moreover, whoever stored his wealth and sealed it by work of magic, has, supposedly, intentionally overdone its concealment. So, why would he leave clues and markers to aid those who want to locate it? And would he publish that in newspapers that would reveal information about his hidden treasure to people of all regions and in all horizons? This would contradict the intent of concealment.

Furthermore, acts of rational persons are necessarily for beneficial purposes. Whoever stores money does so for his children, relatives, or for whoever inherits them. No reasonable person would intend to fully and completely conceal it from everybody and instead intend it for sport or destruction or leave it to someone he does not know at all—someone who would come from distant nations—this would not be the intent of any rational person under any circumstance.

Some might ask: Where is the wealth of the nations that came before us, which is known to have been abundant and large?

In response, know that wealth in the form of gold, silver, jewelry, and other luxurious properties are in fact precious metals and earned tokens like iron, copper, lead, and any other real property or precious metals. The difference is that intense urbanization emphasizes the value of these metals through human work, causing their value to increase and decrease. What is found in the hands of people is exchanged and inherited. It is possible that such precious metals are transferred from a region to another and from a state to another depending on their utility and their exchange rate.[46]

Urban living invites the dynamic adoption of precious metals that would allow for the exchange of goods between regions. For instance, if the amount of money decreases in *al-Maghrib* (Northwest Africa) and *Ifrīqiyya* (modern day Tunisia), it will not decrease in Slovanian (*Saqāliba*) and Frankian (*ifranj*) countries. And if it decreases in Egypt and the Levant (*Sham*), it will not decrease in India and China. The monetary value of such precious metals is a function of machinery, earnings, and urbanization. These are the factors that will cause their abundance or their scarcity. That, in addition to the fact that precious metals (*ma`ādin*) are subjected to wear-and-tear like all existing things, which affects pearls and gems faster than it affects other minerals.

Similarly, gold, silver, copper, iron, lead, and tin are also affected by wear-and-tear, which could destroy their value in a very short time.

As for Egypt being known for people seeking treasures, the cause for that is the fact that in Egypt, since its fall under the control of the Copts for a thousand years or more years, they used to bury their dead along with their possessions of gold, silver, gems, and pearls, in line with the customs of the people who ruled over Egypt before them. So, when the last dynasty of the Copts ended and when control over Egypt fell to the Persians, the latter dynasty searched the graves for such precious metals, and they discovered indescribable amounts in royal graves in the Pyramids and other burial sites. The Greeks had done the same—transforming their graves into attraction sites for treasure hunters until this time. It turned out that much buried wealth was found in these graves many times.

The known fact about Copts burying their dead with money, or honoring their dead by leaving with them valuable containers and caskets made out of gold and silver designed for these purposes, rendered Coptic graves suspected locations of such valuable objects for thousands of years. For this reason, the people of Egypt were interested in searching for these sought items because they actually

---

[46] When a different word appears in a different edition of the Arabic text, I often include both meanings, especially if both meanings fit the context. Here, the main manuscript I used included the word *aghrāḍ*; in another manuscript, the word *a`wāḍ* was used instead. I opted to keep both meanings.

existed in the graves, and they were able to extract it. This was true to the extent that when the last dynasty categorized taxed items, it included taxes on people who extracted such treasures.

Moreover, those who were employed as treasure hunters, who were foolish and delusional, were also taxed as well. Thus, greedy bureaucrats who were also interested in these treasures found taxation to be a promising way to continue their quest by putting the idea in the heads of such fools. Nonetheless, all their efforts were unsuccessful. We seek God's refuge from such perdition. And we recommend that those who were afflicted by these whispers (*waswasa*) must take refuge in God from their inability to make a living and their laziness in seeking to make a living, just as the Messenger of God took refuge from it and turned away from the ways and delusions of Satan. They should not occupy themselves with absurdities and untrue stories. "And God provides subsistence to whoever wishes without accounting."

5. On the Benefits of *Jāh* and Wealth

We deduce that social standing (*jāh*) is beneficial financially from the fact that we find that wealthy and fortunate persons from some types of vocations are in much better financial conditions than people who lacked social standing (*fāqid al-jāh*). The reason for this is that the person of standing is served by acts intended for gaining proximity to such a person,[47] whose shadow is sought and whose social standing is needed. People end up helping him with their work in all of his needs, be it necessary or auxiliary. Consequently, the value of all that work is added to his earnings and all of his endeavors will be paid for as compensation for work performed by people who did not require pay. And this causes an increase in the value of his own businesses. In this case, he would be profiting from the value of earned labor and other values associated with unearnable labor of others,[48] thus increasing his profit.

Working for a person of high social standing takes many forms, adding value to wealth in the shortest amount of time and as the days go by. Such a person would increase his wealth and his living conditions will be made much easier. Defined as such, it becomes clear why political leadership (*imāra*) is one of the forms of making a living, as we said already. He who has no social standing whatsoever, even if he were a wealthy person, the ease of his conditions (*yasar*) is only equal to his wealth and proportional to his efforts (*sa`y*), and these persons are the majority of merchants (*tujjār*). For this reason, you find that those among them who have social standing (*jāh*) are in much better financial conditions (*aysar bikathīr*).

---

47 Themself

48 Similar to Ibn Khaldun's previous insistence that only living individuals can "make a living," and that earning a living is an *active* endeavor, his purpose here is to critically interrogate the idea that *jāh* is a kind of work. His reasoning, as he explains, is that the individuals who brown-nose to people with *jāh* are actually doing work for them, adding value to the person with *jāh*, who is essentially getting work for free—which Ibn Khaldun is adamant is not real work. From a systems perspective, energy moving through this system that gives clout to people with *jāh* and increases their status is energy unaccounted for; it will, he suggests, have consequences over time.

Further evidence for this can be deduced from the fact that many jurists and scholars of religious and worship matters, if they become widely known, people will hold them in high regard and goodwill to the extent that the people would believe that God would want them supported (*irfādihim*), bringing many people to willfully and sincerely help them with their worldly needs and watch over their interests, which would bring these individuals swift wealth and they become well-off without acquired money, except that resulting from the value of the labor of the helping people.[49] We have seen many examples of this in many regions and countries.

In rural areas, however, they are approached by farmers and merchants and others, while he, the person of social standing (*jāh*), is sitting in his house never leaving it, yet his money keeps increasing and his earnings become greater—thus the rich person becomes richer without effort. He who is not aware of this secret would be surprisingly amazed by his growing wealth and the causes of his riches and the fortunate circumstances; and God almighty provides subsistence (*yarzuq/yarziq*) to whoever wills it without account.

[49] That is, the wealth of people with *jāh* comes from the labor of the people who help them.

6. On How Happiness and Wealth Come Easily to the Subservient and Sycophantic

Being subservient and sycophantic are some of the traits that may lead to happiness.

We have already stated that the earnings that benefit human beings are the value of their work. In a case where a person is fully unemployable and unemployed, such a person will be incomeless in every sense of the word. Moreover, a person's estimated economic worth is proportional to the value of his work, to the respect for his vocation, and to people's need for his product or service. The growth or decline of his earnings are proportional to these said factors.

Additionally, we have previously explained that the social standing of a person benefits his wealth since such a person of high social standing (*jāh*) is sought by people, seeking proximity to him with their own wealth and works for the purposes of avoiding harm and attracting benefits for themselves. Their proximity to a person of high social standing through work or money is thus a substitute for profit that might be generated from their work on investment otherwise deployed—*jāh* in this context is a value enhancer on its own. At the same time, the person of high standing (*jāh*) also benefits from this proximity-driven work and money increasing his wealth and net worth in the fastest time possible.

Social standing (and/or prestige) (*jāh*) is variedly distributed among people, ordered in different degrees distinguishing one class of people from another, with a king holding the highest social standing; no one has power over them. Those who can neither harm nor benefit anyone hold the lowest social standing. And the space between these two social ranks is occupied by many social classes of different social standings. The work of God's wisdom in his creation ensures that their livelihood is regulated, their welfare is secured, and their continued existence (*baqā'uhum*) is realized, for the existence and persistence of the human species can only be realized through the cooperation of all its members for the sake of their mutual interests. This is so, for it has been determined that a single human being could not exist by himself, and even if it were to happen, which is rare, his continued existence would not be tenable.

Moreover, such cooperation would not take place without coercion. Most of them are ignorant of the welfare their kind (human species). And they are ignorant of the fact that human actions are outcomes of thinking and reflection, not outcomes of their nature (biology). The individual might refuse to cooperate, and this would require forcing him to cooperate, for it is necessary that the enforcer, who would coerce members of his species to do what their collective welfare requires of them, is enacting a fulfilment of divine wise design that ensures the continued existence of the species. This is the meaning of God's statement: "And we have raised some of them over others by some degrees so that they may employ one another for your God's mercy is better than whatever they hoard."[50]

Therefore, it is clear that social standing (*jāh*) is the will enabling human beings to manage those under their control from amongst their species both through permission and denial, and through power by force and dominance; to enable them to defend against harm and to secure their benefits through the administration of justice through laws and politics and to employ them for his needs outside that framework.

However, the former (permission/denial) is intended by the divine care towards the self, and the latter is included into it as incidental, like all other bad things that are part of the divine will. For much good (*khayr kathīr*) will not exist without the existence of a little bad (*sharr yasīr*) for material purposes.

[50] *Warafa`na ba`dahum fawqa ba`din darajatin liyattakhidha ba`duhum ba`dan sakhriyan, wa-rahmatu rabbika khayrun mimma yajma`un.*

The good does not bypass the presence of the bad. Rather, it overwhelms that which contains the little bad. This is the meaning of the occurrence of injustice among the created and thus it should be understood.

Each class from the social classes of urban dwellers, be it of a city or of a region, has power over the classes below it. Each member of a lower class seeks the support of a person of high social standing (*jāh*) from a higher class, and such a person will augment his earnings through the use of people from the social class below his, proportionally to the benefit gained from seeking the proximity to the person with *jāh*. Therefore, the *jāh* is involved in all activities related to making a living and the *jāh* widens and narrows based on social class and the stage occupied by its holder. If the *jāh* is wide, the benefit emanating from it will be so; if it is a little narrow, the same.

A *jāh*-less person, even if he has money, his ease (*yasaruh*) will be proportional to his work or to his money and the rate of his effort (*sa`y*) coming and going, developing (*tanmiya*) it like most merchants and farmers in most cases.

Similarly, masters of *ṣanā'i`*, if they have no *jāh* and are restricted to the profits of their *ṣanā'i`*, they will likely gravitate towards poverty and indigence, and they do not quickly become wealthy. They make only a bare living, just fending off the distress of poverty.

Should *jāh* be as we described above, and that *jāh* is derivable, and that happiness and good (*khayr*) are connected to acquiring *jāh*, know then, that offering its benefits and spending it should be one of the greatest joys and most honorable of them all; such spending should not be to benefit those seeking it, but it should be spent on those under their control—this way the spending will done from a position of power and with dignity, requiring its seeker to be subservient and flattering as if asking kings and dignitaries; otherwise the *jāh* cannot be obtained.

For this reason, we said that subservience (*khuḍū`)* and flattery (*tamalluq*) are some of the effects of acquiring such *jāh,* that is a condition for acquiring happiness and earnings for most happy and wealthy people, through *tamalluq.* For this reason, we find that most people whose character is marked by dignity and aloofness (*taraffu`*) and high view of oneself (*shimam*) do not acquire *jāh,* thus limiting their income from their work, and they slide towards poverty and need. One should know that such aloofness (*taraffu`*), which are some of the ill-spoken-of (*madhmūma*) traits, are acquired because such a person has the illusion of perfection and that people need his goods or services, like the scholar who is versed in his science and the writer who is skilled in his writing, or the eloquent poet confident in his poetry, and every other skilled craftsman who thinks that people are in need to what he has to offer. And this would make him act as if he is above their level (*taraffu`*) due to his belief in the high value of his service or product.

Similarly, people of familial connection to established names are aloof. Among this class of people is one who is connected to ancestors who were kings or famous scientists or who have a complete archive on which they base their narratives about what they heard or was told from the men of their past in the city. They would erroneously feel entitled to the same treatment and the same rewards as their ancestors due to their affinity to them and their inheritance of them. They are, at present, holding on to a void matter (*al-amr al-ma`dūm*).

The same applies to people of experience, ideas, and wisdom. Some of them would falsely believe (*yatawahham*) a sense of completeness in themselves and being needed by others. You would find that all people of this type, all of them, have a high regard for themselves (*mutaraffi`īn),* they do not subordinate (*yakhḍa`*) themselves to a person with *jāh*; they do not flatter (*tamalluq*) persons who are higher than them, and they belittle (*yastasghirūn*) everyone other than themselves due their belief that they are better than people. Such a person would find it beneath them to subordinate (*al-khuḍū`*) themselves to even the king—he would consider doing so intimidating (*madhalla*), diminutive (*hawānan*), and dishonest (*safhan*). He would judge people for their dealings with him according to what he falsely believes (*yatawahham*) and he would hold a grudge (*yaḥqid*) against anyone who treats him less than he falsely thinks (*yatawahham*) he deserves. Perhaps anxiety and sadness would strike such person's soul, because of his belief that he is treated less than he deserves, and he continues to greatly struggle in attempting to extract justice for himself or resenting people even more.

People, too, will come to resent him because humans are egotistic by nature. Rarely will one of them concede perfection (*kamāl*) and aloofness (*taraffu`*) to another unless through some kind of force (*qahr*), dominance (*ghalaba*), and overbearing (*istiṭāla*)—all of which are part of *jāh*.

Therefore, if a person has these traits but lacks *jāh*, and he clearly lacks it as we explained, people will hate him (*maqatahu al-nās*) because of this transcendence (*taraffu`*) and he will not receive any of their sympathy. Consequently, losing the *jāh* from the social class higher than his due to the hate (*maqt*)—resulting in his exclusion from sitting in their circles and visiting their homes, leading to the ruin of his pension and staying in poverty (*faqr*) and need (*khaṣāṣa*), or barely above that.

As to wealth, such a person will never be able to obtain it in the first place. It is based on these facts that popular wisdom states that he with complete knowledge (*kāmil al-ma`rifa*) lacks luck (*ḥaḍḍ*; wealth), for he is rewarded for what he earned in the form of knowledge (*ma`rifa*), which diminishes what he would otherwise earn through luck (*ḥaḍḍ*; wealth). The meaning of this proverb is what we just explained above.

Whoever is created for a specific thing, it shall be made easy for him.[51] And God is the power holder; no God but Him.

In some countries, it may happen that there is a disconnection between the character traits and social rank, in that some from

[51] *Wa-man khuliqa li-shay'in yussira lah.*

the low ranks may rise and some of the high ranks may decline as a result of such disconnection. This happens when a political order has reached its limit dominating and usurping, At such a stage, the ruling clan would claim royal and governmental authority exclusively for itself. All others would despair, losing any hope in governing. Rather, they all fall to a rank below that of the king and under the power of the Sultan, as if they were authorized to belong to him. When the State (*dawla*) continues and royal power flourishes, those who seek proximity to the Sultan, through advice or work, will become all equal but beneath him, and will be employed by him, given from his wealth, to do many of his things needing attention.

You will find many common people seek the proximity of the Sultan by offering counsel and all kinds of services, cajoling him; using all forms of submissiveness and flattery toward the Sultan, his entourage, and his family, so that eventually they will be firmly entrenched, and the ruler will admit them into his circle. Their proximity to power brings them a great deal of happiness.

Over time, the descendants of such people would not submit and lower themselves before the Sultan. They would not do the same as their ancestors, falsely thinking (*mughtarrīn*) that what their fathers had done would bring them recognition without them doing the same. These children would then try to benefit from the achievements of their fathers without using the resources of the State. The Sultan will hate them for it, and he will remove them from his circle of close associates. The Sultan would then prefer the self-made ones who do not seek to profit from the past, who do not want to prove anything and who do not think too highly of themselves (*taraffu`*). Instead, they would embrace toadyism and submissiveness, and they would seek his hiring of them to do his work, which increases their social standing (*jāh*) and raises their rank. They would be sought out by other people seeking favors due their proximity to the Sultan and their standing with him.

The children of the first generation, on the other hand, still thinking highly of themselves and their reliance on the past—their attitude will only bring them more distance from the Sultan and more of his dislike (*maqt*); while the pretenders rise above them until the State goes extinct (*tanqariḍ al-dawla*). This is the natural path of the State and its connection to the pretenders (*mustani`īn*) in all likelihood; and God almighty knows best, and by Him we succeed, no Lord other than Him.

7. On Persons in Charge of Religious Affairs including Judges, Muftis, Teachers, Imams, Preachers, and Mu'azzins

Persons employed in the religious affairs such as judges, muftis, teachers, prayer leaders, preachers, muazzins, and the like—their wealth, in all likelihood, will not be great. The reason for this is that, as we have stated before, earned income is the value realized from a person's vocational activities (work). The value of work differs depending on the need for such work. In an urban setting, if such work is necessary and sought by the public, the work's value will be greater and the need for it will be even stronger.

The people specializing in religious professions are not sought by the public. Rather, they are needed by private segment of society (*khawāṣṣ*) who practice their religion. And when a religious decree (*fatwa*) or arbitration of a conflict are needed, their service is not necessary as a public service still; that is, it is not a general service to the public (*`umūm*)—and they[52] can be unemployed in most cases. The leader of the State, however, might be interested in them officiating certain matters given the leader's interest in public welfare, and in return, the leader would allocate a share for their subsistence proportional to his needs for them as we explained.

The leader would not equate them to people who have power or to craftsmen, from the point of view of religion and official business, but he would reward them based on the public's need for their services and the need of the urban dwellers, and that would amount to very little.

Moreover, because their service is noble, they carry themselves with pride before the people and feel proud of themselves. Therefore, they are not obsequious to persons of rank (*jāh*) to obtain something to augment their subsistence. In fact, they would not

[52] These religious professionals.

have time for that, given that they are occupied with those noble things they have to offer, and which consist of exerting both the mind and the body. In fact, the noble character of the profession does not allow them to market themselves to people interested in their services; they are above that. Therefore, in all likelihood, their wealth would not reach a huge level.

I discussed this with some renowned persons, and they disagreed with me about my findings. Then, I came across some old leaves from the account books of the government offices in the palace of al-Ma'mūn. I read in them some information about income and expenditures including the salaries of judges, prayer leaders, and muezzins. I shared this information with one of the people I had the discussion with, He reviewed it, too, and found that what I told him was correct. We were both astonished at the secret ways of God with regard to His creation and His wisdom concerning His worlds. God is the Creator, the Able; no Lord besides Him.

8. On Agriculture

Agriculture is a way of making a living for the meek and healthy people from among the rural dwellers. Because agriculture is rooted in nature from the point of view of products and simple in terms of procedure, in all likelihood, it is not undertaken by urban dwellers or spendthrifts. Those who take agriculture for a vocation are characterized by timidity and meekness. When Prophet Muhammad (P)[53] saw a plowshare (*sikka*) in one of the houses of the people of Madina (*Anṣār*), he said: "Whenever such a thing enters the home of a community, timidity (and humiliation; *dhull*)) will accompany it." al-Bukhari explained that it applies to excess in reliance on the tool. He provided a section in which he warned against the use of the plowshare (*sikka*) or exceeding the limit set for it.

God knows best, but it would seem that the reason for this attitude towards owning a *sikka* might be that it is often connected to mortgage that would control the life of the borrower and give the upper hand to the lender. In such an arrangement, the borrower is forced into a life of timidity and wretchedness at the hands of lenders, exerting crushing coercive force and oppression.

The Prophet Muhammad (P) said: "The End of Time will not arrive until alms-giving (*zakā*) becomes mortgaged," a reference to the tyrannical ruler who coerces the people, who becomes domineering, unjust, forgetful to the divine laws governing investment and development, and who considers laws, all laws (*ḥuqūq*), to be a form of debt due to kings and states.

And God almighty knows more and by Him we succeed.

---

[53] As is the case with Muslim authors, the name of Prophet Muhammad is always followed by the deferential statement, "May God's Prayers and Pease be upon him," abbreviated in Arabic text by a calligraphic icon. We use (P) in this English translation.

9. On Trade: Meaning, Methods, and Types

Know that trade (*tijāra*) means the attempt to earn money (*kasb*) by augmenting capital (*tanmiyat a-māl*) through the buying of merchandise (*al-sila`*) at a cheap price (*rukhṣ*) and selling it at an expensive price (*ghalā'*), whatever merchandise it might be: flour (*daqīq*),[54] crop (*zar`*), animal (*ḥayawān*), or fabric (*qumāsh*). The amount representing the difference between cost (buying price) and selling price is called gain (*ribḥ*).

A merchant attempting to make such a gain may store the merchandise and monitor the market's[55] condition (*ḥawālat al-aswāq*) as it gravitates from cheap to expensive prices, which would augment his gain. Alternatively, a merchant may transport his merchandise to another country where people would pay more for it—more than they would pay in his own country for the same merchandise and where he bought them, also augmenting his gain (*ribḥ*). To illustrate, when expert merchants are asked to explain the secrets of trade (*tijāra*), they would say, "I will teach it to you in two words: buying the cheap (*al-rakhīṣ*) and selling the expensive (*al-ghālī*)." This anecdote establishes the definition we just presented. And God Almighty knows best and with God comes success.

[54] In Rosethal's translation, the list included "slaves." No manuscript consulted for this translation referenced slaves. It is possible that the translator misread the word *daqīq*, (which in North African Arabic, at least, refers to flour), as the classical Arabic word *raqīq*, which may mean, among other things, slaves.

[55] In this translation I have used "the market" to signify the broader market of buying, selling, and trading. However, it is worthwhile noting that Ibn Khaldun's original text translates directly to plural "markets," indicating that a merchant or trader would monitor not only the local market but regional and international markets as well.

10. On the Characteristics of Merchants

In this section, we discuss which kind of people take trade (*tijāra*) for a profession and which people should avoid the trade profession.

We have already defined trade (*tijāra*) as the increase of capital by buying merchandise and attempting to sell it at a price higher than the buying price (cost), either by monitoring the conditions of the markets, by transporting it to a country where such merchandise sells at higher prices, or by selling it at high prices through fixed time periods.[56]

The gain, compared to the principal capital, might be small. However, if the capital used in the trade is large so will be the gain, because the little in a lot is a lot.[57] In such an investment business, attempting to increase capital through such gains, money has to reach the hands of merchants who buy and sell goods. They have to negotiate selling and buying prices. Fair-minded persons are few in this business. Deception, talking down the merchandise before buying it to reduce its sale price, and bidding up the price of the merchandise when selling it to increase the selling price all have an impact on the gain (*ribḥ*). Add to that having to deal with time-fixed loans, which are connected to investment terms; denial of the amount of capital invested and the terms of the investment when there is no written agreement or witnesses; and the cost of arbitration, which is often decided based on circumstantial evidence, all these factors make merchants struggle and make them go through trying conditions. Merchants often secure little gains with much effort and hardship. And in some cases, even the little gain will not be realized, or capital may be lost.

[56] Ibn Khaldun is describing time as a system for generating wealth, more of an active tool that a merchant can use rather than time simply passing. The Arabic text refers to time as a variable that can be fixed to achieve a specific outcome.
[57] *al-qalīlu fī al-kathīri kathīr.*

Therefore, if he is a capable adversary, sharp in accounting, a skilled negotiator, and connected to the ruler, he may have a fair chance for success given these traits in him. Otherwise, he would need social standing (*jāh*) for a shield. Having a social standing (*jāh*) will bring him respectability among fellow traders and merchants and force the rulers to treat him fairly when his cases come before them. His wealth will be fairly secure by default in the first instance and forced in the former.

He who lacks initiative (*jur'a*) and who is not forthcoming (*miqdām*), and lacks social standing (*jāh*), such a person should stay away from trade for he will be risking his wealth. Sellers will feast on his wealth, and he will not have a fair shake. This would be the case for what is more likely in people, especially the public and the sellers, is that they have great appetite for what is in the hands of other people, seeking it like a wild animal pursuing prey. If it were not for the laws acting as a deterrent (*wāzi`*), people's money would have been usurped (*nahb*). "If it were not for God using some people against each, earth will be corrupted (*fasadat*); however, God has provided for all."

11. On the Ethics of Merchants

In this section we will show that the ethics of merchants are lower than the ethics of nobles and kings. This is the case because merchants, generally, deal with buying and selling. Cunning (*mukāyasa*) is necessary for this line of work. So, when a merchant exclusively relies on cunning, cunning becomes his exclusive trait. The quality of cunning, which we mean here, is far from nobility, which is the ethics of kings and nobles (*ashrāf*; persons of eminence).

When one seeks timidity and humility (*istirthāl*), a characteristic of the lower class of merchants, including quarrelsomeness, cheating, defrauding, committing perjury when rejecting and accepting statements concerning prices, such ethics can be expected and can reach the lowest point based on what is known.

For this reason, leaders avoid being involved in such profession to avoid acquiring such ethics. There may exist some merchants who remain free of such ethics and who are able to avoid them, due to their seeking eminence on their own and nobility in their character; but such persons are very rare in existence. And God guides whom He wills by His generosity and providence, and He is the Lord of those who came before and those who came after.

12. On the Merchant's Transportation of Merchandise

The merchant who knows his business will move only merchandise that is needed by all—the rich and poor, rulers and commoners alike—for only through such high demand will his merchandise sell out. But if a merchant specializes in moving merchandise that appeals to the needs of only some people, then it may not be possible for all of his merchandise to sell out, since people making up his main market may, for some reason or another, find it difficult to buy it. His business would, then, slump and he would make no profit.

Similarly, in relation to transporting (exporting) merchandise that is needed, a merchant would export the average kind of it only, for the high end of each kind of merchandise is sought by rich people and the State's bureaucrats and they are few. The public will be interested, due to need, in the average quality of each type and on that the merchant would focus his attention because that will determine selling out of all his merchandise or spoiling it.

Likewise, importing merchandise from far away countries or through dangerous trade routes can be more profitable for merchants and produce greater gains, and be less dependent on the conditions of the markets because exported and imported goods are of limited quantities because they are produced in distant lands and because of the great risk and fewer people willing to transport them. And all of that makes them scarce and when you say scarce, it implies high prices.

On the other hand, when the country is near and the routes are safe for traveling, there will be many to transport the goods. Thus, they will be found in larger quantities, and the prices will be lower.

Case in point, merchants who dare to enter the Sudan countries are the most prosperous and wealthy of all people. The distance and the difficulty of the roads they travel are great. They must cross a difficult desert which is made nearly inaccessible by fear of danger and beset by threat of thirst. Water is found there only in a few known spots, known only to caravan guides. Such a road is then taken by only a few people who can handle the distance. For these reasons, merchandise of the Sudan countries are scarce in our country, making them particularly expensive. The same applies to our merchandise sold in their countries. Thus, exported and imported merchandises become more valuable, making these merchants rich quickly and increasing their wealth. The same applies to merchants who travel great distances from our country to the East. As for those who travel back and forth between the cities and regions of one country, they earn little and make insignificant gains due to the abundance of merchandise in large quantities and the availability of a larger number of people willing to transport it. And God provides subsistence; the Mighty powerful.

13. On Hoarding

Common wisdom among experienced and reflective persons popularized the view that hoarding (*iḥtikār*) agricultural goods (*zar`*) awaiting the time of high prices is inauspicious and that, in the long run, it brings to one's profit spoilage and loss. The reason for this, and God knows best, is that people need food, and with food being a necessity, they must spend money to secure it. When they do, they become emotionally attached to that money because humans tend to be protective and attached to that which they own. Such an attachment somehow has great effect on those who take it away from them for nothing. Hoarding the needed food is recognized by the Lawgiver (*shāri`*; God) as taking money from people through falsehood. It is true that selling hoarded goods is not taking things for free (*majānan*). However, because humans are emotionally attached to their money, paying large sums of it for ordinary goods that happen to be a necessity just because someone hoarded it is a form of coercion.

Other than foodstuffs and victuals, which are basic necessities for people, things do not fall under the hoarding rule because such items are sought by those who crave pleasure and such people who choose and insist on paying for them. These individuals are not attached to the money they spent on such goods more than their attachment to the goods they desired (*shahwa*).

For these reasons, a person who is known to be a hoarder will be haunted by the force of the souls (*quwwa nafsāniyya*) pursuing justice for what he took from them; such pursuit will result in the corruption of his gains. And God knows better.

Related to this, I heard a funny and curious story from the learned community of *al-Maghrib* (*mashyakhat al-maghrib*). Shaykh Abu Abdallah al-Abli said:

> I was in the house of the judge in Fez, during the reign of Sultan Abu Sa`id—and he is the jurist Abul-

Hasan al-Mlili. He was offered to choose the branch of revenue bureau from which his salary would be paid. He thought carefully then said: From the taxes collected on wine (*khamr*). Those present were amused, reacting with laughter. Curious about his answer, they asked him about the wisdom behind his choice. He replied: "Since all forms of taxes are *ḥarām* (blameworthy), I am choosing money to which the soul of its giver is attached. And on wine, rarely a person would spend money unless they are happy and cheerful by its effects, rarely sorry for spending the money on it, and rarely is his soul attached to it.

This is a curious observation. And God knows the secrets of the hearts.

14. On the Effects of Cheap Prices

Cheap prices are harmful to merchants who specialize in sales of items with discounted prices. The reason being, as we have stated before, earnings (*kasb*) and making a living (*ma`āsh*) are derived from the work of people with skills and expertise in doing something (*ṣanā'i`*) or from commerce (*tijāra*). Commerce means the buying of merchandise and goods, storing them, and waiting for the right market conditions (*ḥawālat al-aswāq*) that bring about an increase in their prices. The price difference is called gain (*ribḥ*).

Those perpetually employed in commerce may collect earnings (*kasb*) and make a living (*ma`āsh*) from such a profession. However, when the price of one kind of merchandise remains low for a long period of time, or the interest in any edible, wearable, or improvable[58] thing drops, and when the market's conditions are not as favorable as the merchant hoped, his gains and investments will be compromised over the length of time. The market for that specific merchandise, too, will slump, adding more trouble to merchants, forcing them to stop their activities, and that would destroy their capital.

To understand the connection between low price of a single kind of merchandise and the economy, consider an agricultural product (*zar`*): If the price of such an agricultural product stays sustainably low over a long period of time, the conditions of all those employed in the varies stages, like those engaged in farming and growing, will be harmed due to the reduction in gains (profit; *ribḥ*), its scarcity, or absence. This would lead to lack of, or reduced return on, investments, forcing them to spend more money on their invested capital, leading them to poor financial conditions and poverty. Moreover, those employed in flour processing, baking, and all areas of employment connected to grain, for example, from the

[58] I used this term to translate *mutamawal `alā al-jumla*, which I believe is a reference to added-value items: things that are bought in bulk or in large amounts, and then reprocessed or repackaged and resold individually.

moment it is put in the ground to the moment it is eaten, will be affected also. Furthermore, the soldier or the security officer whose salary might be coming from the taxes imposed by the king on people employed in grain-growing and processing, they, too, will experience problems with their subsistence; forcing them to stop doing their work.

The same applies to perpetual low prices of sugar or honey, which will influence all that is connected to these goods, should the merchants specializing in the sale of these products stop their work.

The same applies to persisting low prices of clothes; it will have a negative impact on all the people employed in the sector; too high of prices could result in the same thing, as well.

Earnings and subsistence of people is linked to the averaging of prices and in the speedy fluctuation of markets; the science for this is connected to the management of revenues among urban dwellers.

People are generally happy with low prices in agricultural products, compared to all other goods, because everyone needs food, rich and poor. Those needing help (poor) are a majority among urban dwellers, so care plays a major role here, favoring subsistence over trade in this particular kind of product (foodstuffs). Indeed, God is the provider, the reliably powerful; and God almighty is the Lord of the Great Universe.

15. On the Ethics of Merchants

Merchants' ethics are inferior to those of leaders, and they are the furthest from chivalry (*murū'a*).[59]

In the preceding section, I introduced the idea that merchants are compelled to grapple with the difficulties associated with buying, selling, and producing gains and profits. For this, a merchant must face cunning, cleverness, quarreling, and willingness to enter into disputes—these are the hazards of this profession. These qualities diminish intelligence and chivalry and injure the latter's virtues because acts must affect the soul.[60] Good deeds (*af`āl al-khayr*) make a person good and smart and bad deeds (*af'āl al-sharr*) and nonsense (*safsafa*) have the opposite effect. These bad, acquired traits, should they be instilled first and repeated (*sabiqat wa-takarrarat*), will take hold of the person and endure; but will be diminished only if preceded by encultured good due to the imprinting of blameworthy effects in the soul[61]—as is the case with all abilities acquired through actions.[62]

These effects will vary depending on the kind of trade and the stage they are in. Those who are in the low stage, who associate closely with bad traders, who cheat and defraud and perjure themselves when denying and confirming prices, the impact of those ethics on him will be strongest. He will be dominated by deceitfulness, and he would be farthest from chivalry (*murū'a*) and will never be able to acquire it. In the best scenario, his chivalry could be affected

---

[59] I used chivalry to translate the word *murū'a* not because it matches in meaning, but because it is similar in that it contains many descriptors and adjectives that are hardly possible to capture through a single word. It references desirable traits in benevolent leaders and influencers, like justice, honor, courage, fairness, courtesy, and willingness, and readiness to help the vulnerable.

[60] This seems to be a prescriptive, not descriptive statement: *al-af'āl labudda min `awdati athariha `alā al-nafs*.

[61] Although (potentially undesirable) traits a person acquires due to their profession will endure within them, any encultured good that took hold before a person acquired these traits will temper the potentially undesirable traits. This is the reason that early enculturing of goodness is important: Without it, acquired traits can go so far as to affect one's soul. For someone who was not initially encultured with goodness, the acquired traits will be permanent traits, as there are no other forces to work against them.

[62] *Al-malakāt nāshi'a `an al-af'āl.*

by the constant cunning and quibbling, which can destroy it. The other kind of merchants are those who shield themselves with *jāh*, protecting themselves from the effects of the traits encultured among merchants, but such merchants are very rare or less-than-rare.

The existence of such a merchant who preserves his noble character is rare because for that to happen, he must end up with a large sum of money at once through a curious type (*naw` gharīb*) of event, or he must inherit it from someone in his household. He could use this obtained wealth to connect with the people of the state, which will provide him with exposure and fame among his contemporaries. He would then become above engaging himself directly in trade. Instead, he would pay his entourage and his agents to do the work for him. Rulers will treat him fairly in applying their laws to him, due to their trust in his fairness and care, holding him above the traits associated with merchants, due to his distance from the actions associated with the trade we mentioned.

Their *murū'a* will become firmer and far from argumentations except the effect of what might occur behind the veil when dealing with their agents and their associates who manage their trade business and augment their wealth for them. However, because dealing with agents and associates is less frequent then dealing with other merchants and customers, the effects of the actions associated with the trade is minuscule, making its effect insignificant. And God created you and what you do.

16. On Acquiring *Ṣanā'i`*

Ṣanā'i`*[63] must be acquired through science. For it should be known that a *ṣinā`a[64] is an ability (*malaka*) to do something that might be conceptual and practical, requiring doing and thinking. Because it is practical, it follows that it is concrete, corporeal, and perceptible by the senses. Transfer of corporeal matters that is perceptible is done through direct practice, for doing so would make it more comprehensively and more perfectly improved, because direct practice is more beneficial.

The ability (*malaka*) is an enduring quality that is acquired by repeating the specific action over and over until it is firmly formed. How much of the original ability is transferred will determine the level of ability.[65] Transfer of knowledge through firsthand observation (*mu`āyana*) is more comprehensive and more complete than the transfer of information and scientific rules about it from distance. Ability gained through instructional information, careful teaching, and the ability of the mentor all contribute to the proficiency of the mentee and the development of his ability (*malakātih*).

Moreover, some *ṣanā'i`* are simple and some others are complex. The simple *ṣanā'i`* specialize in necessities(*ḍarūrīyyāt*). Complex *ṣanā'i`*, on the other hand, focus on luxuries. The simple *ṣanā'i* are taught first because they are simple and there are many reasons for such skills to be transferred. As such, these are learned first and because they are learned first, the learning is not complete. Through conceptualization of different types and different additions, from theory to practice, through deductive reasoning, the *ṣinā`a* would gradually evolve towards perfection and completeness.

---

[63] What persons are trained to do as a profession/vocation.
[64] Singular of *ṣanā'i`*.
[65] *Wa-`alā nisbati al-aṣli takūnu al-malaka.*

Attaining such level of perfection does not happen in one shot, especially in matters related to manufacturing, for it requires time. For this reason, in small countries, *ṣanā'i`* are incomplete and simple. Once the cities of a country increase in size and demand for luxury items increases, engaging in *ṣanā'i`* will transition from what could be potentially (*quwwa*) done to what is actually (*fi`l*) done perfectly.

Ṣanā'i`* are further divided into those which are connected to making a living, be they necessary or not, and those which are connected to ideas (*afkār*), which are the specialties of human beings including sciences, *ṣanā'i`, and politics. In the first category, we can include tailorship (*ḥiyāka*), butchery (*jazāra*), carpentry (*nijāra*), ironwork (*ḥidāda*), and their like. In the second category, we can include bookmanship (*al-wirāqa*), which is the labor in bookmaking including copying and archiving; singing, poetry, teaching sciences, and their like. In the third category, we can include serving in the military (*jundiyya*) and its like. And God knows more.

17. On *Ṣanā'i`* and Urbanization

The perfection of *ṣanā'i`* is connected to the perfection and the size of urban living. The reason being that people, as long as they do not achieve urban living and as long as their cities are not modernized, then they will be concerned only with the necessities of living (*ma`āsh*), which consist of obtaining materials of sustenance like wheat and others. However, when the city is modernized, when work opportunities become abundant, and provides for all the necessities and still has a surplus, such surplus will be spent on luxury items for luxury living (*ma`āsh al-rafah*).

Ṣanā'i`* and sciences belong to humans due their ability to think (*fikr*), which distinguishes humans from animals. Food, as an animalistic and nutritional imperative, is necessary and takes priority over sciences and *ṣanā'i`, which are of lower priority compared to food. The level of refinement of *ṣanā'i`* and the quality of products of *ṣanā'i`* are intimately connected to the level urbanization in the country. This is the case because it is in urban living that accumulation of wealth and spendthriftness[66] are common. In rural living or less dense living, on the other hand, there is a need for only simple *ṣanā'i`*, especially *ṣanā'i`* needed for producing necessities including the work of the carpenter, ironsmith, tailor, shoemaker, and butcher. And when such *ṣanā'i`* exist still, they are neither perfect nor done well. They exist in the form and quality required by need, for they are all of intermediate purpose, not intended to be end-products for their own sake.

However, when urbanization flourishes and the luxuries become in high demand, some of the effects of such urban development would include the refinement and improvement of the *ṣanā'i`*. Consequently, these *ṣanā'i`* become complete and other *ṣanā'i`* would be derived from them, which would encourage

[66] The Arabic word embodies not only spendthriftness but extravagance.

spendthriftness and *ṣanā'i`* that respond to such spendthriftness like the butcher, the tanner, the jeweler, the goldsmith, and the like.

As urbanization flourishes further, these *ṣanā'i`* become even more perfected and refined to their limits, as perfection becomes the goal, becoming a new path of making a living in such a country. In fact, such *ṣanā'i`* become the most profitable activities, due to demand for luxury in the city, creating new professions like the painter, the coppersmith, the bath attendant, the cook, the biscuit baker, the cake baker; the teacher of singing, dancing, and drum beating, etc. Like the bookmakers who pursue the craft of copying, correcting, and binding books, these *ṣanā'i`*, transformed by demand for luxury in the city, become intellectual activities that occupy the mind or something like that. These *ṣanā'i`* can become excessive when urban living becomes excessive. In fact, we learn that among the people of Egypt some people teach dumb creatures like birds and domestic donkeys, who[67] produce marvelous spectacles, practice magic and illusions that trick the eye, teach them how to swing, dance, and walk on ropes in the air, lift heavy objects like animals and rocks; and many other *ṣanā'i`* that do not exist among us in *al-Maghrib*. These *ṣanā'i`* do not exist in the cities of *al-Maghrib* because urbanization herein did not reach the same level of urbanization in Egypt and Cairo. May God make its urbanization with Muslims endure; and God is wise and knowing.

[67] The people who train animals.

18. On what Makes *Ṣanā'i`* Established in a Country

Ṣanā'i`* become established in a country when city-living is established for a long time. The reason for this is obvious. All *ṣanā'i` are customs and habits of urban living. Additionally, customs become established only through much repetition over a long duration. Under such conditions, the manner of the practice becomes encultured and established across generations—as if painting the entire generation with the color of the *ṣinā`a*. Just like paint, once such manner is firmly established, it is difficult to remove it.

Therefore, we find that cities with highly developed city-living, after their urban-living falls back and decreases, in such cities, still, you will find traces of such *ṣanā'i`* that do not exist in other more recently inhabited cities, no matter how large the cities and how abundant the goods are. This is only because manners in those old cities have become well-established and firmly rooted through their long duration and constant repetition—something not yet reached by newly established cities.

The situation in Spain now is a good example of this, since therein we find the blueprints of *ṣanā'i`* as well as the way of life still taking hold, established in all areas where there is demand in every region of the country. It would include building, cooking, all kinds of singing and entertainment, including the use of music instruments, dancing; the laying of carpets in palaces, the deliberate arrangements, the planned construction of homes, the decorations on metal containers, pottery, and all kinds of vessels; the giving of banquets and wedding parties, and all the other *ṣanā'i`* required by luxury-living and its customs. We find them undertaking these activities with much competence and much regularity. The *ṣanā'i`* of such a country took hold among its people and the products of such *ṣanā'i`* are abundant, making them stand out compared to all other countries (*amṣār*)—all that, despite the decrease in its urban living. Many of Spain's cities do not equal the urban living of other countries of *al-`udwa*. This is only because, as we have mentioned before, city-living (*al-ḥaḍar*) had become deeply established amongst them (the Spaniards) through stability provided by the long rule of the Umayyad state (*al-dawla al-umawiyya*), the Gothic dynasty before it, and after it by the sectarian (*ṭawā'if*) states, and so on and so forth.

Consequently, city-living in Spain had reached a level that had not been reached in any other region except, reportedly, in Iraq, Syria, and Egypt—made possible by the long rule of the States there, too. Also, the *ṣanā'i`* became well-established, diverse in form, and perfected in style and quality. The mark (*ṣibgha)* of such *ṣanā'i`* remained firm in those cities never to leave it, until it was totally destroyed—the same way color lasts in the garment.

This was also the case in Tunisia where many cities were established by the states of Sanhajah and Almohads after them, which elevated its *ṣanā'i`* in all areas—though it was below the level attained in *al-Andalus* (Spain). However, *ṣanā'i`* in Tunisia were augmented by design brought from Egypt, given the short distance between the two countries, and due to frequent travels from Tunisia to Egypt every year. Also, Tunisians have lived in Egypt for ages (*`uṣūr*), and then they brought back the luxury customs and technical knowledge that they liked. Thus, their way of life became similar to that of Egypt, for the reasons mentioned; and also, to that of *al-Andalus*, because many people from eastern *al-Andalus*, after leaving (*jalā'*) in the seventh century, settled in Tunisia. Thus, certain aspects of city living have become firmly rooted there, even though its cities at this time were not suitable to them. However, a *ṣibgha,* once established, rarely changes, except when its host ceases to exist. The same applies to the cities of Qayrawan, Marrakech, and Qal`at Ibn Hammad, where remnants of such urban living can be deduced; although these cities are nowadays in ruins or destined to be so. Only observant individuals will pay attention to these places to learn about the *ṣanā'i`* through the artifacts left behind; the same way an erased line in a book can tell a story. And God is "the Creator, the Knowing One."

19. On What Improves Quality and Quantity of *Ṣanā'i`*

Quality of *ṣanā'i`* improves and output increases with increased demand. The reason for this is that a human being cannot allow his work to happen for nothing, for it is the basis of his earnings (*kasb*) and livelihood (*ma`āsh*). In all his lifetime, there is nothing of benefit to him in anything else except in his work. Therefore, he would not spend work on something that does not benefit him in return. If a particular *ṣinā`a* is in demand and large sums are spent on it, then, such a *ṣinā`a* would become a merchandise in of itself, also attracting spending and funding. People in the cities, therefore, put efforts into learning this *ṣinā`a*, deriving from it their subsistence (*ma`āsh*). Inversely, if a particular *ṣinā`a* is not in demand, its market will not be funded and there will be no interest in learning it. As a result, the *ṣinā`a* will be abandoned and would disappear due to neglect. For this reason, it is reported that Ali, may God be pleased with him, said: "The value of every person is tethered to what he does best." This means that the *ṣinā`a* he knows constitutes his value, that is, the value realized from his labor, which is his livelihood (*ma`āsh*).

On this, there is another secret. That *ṣanā'i`* and learning to improve *ṣanā'i`* are sought by the State, for it is the State that funds the market for such *ṣanā'i`* and their improvement. *Ṣanā'i`* not in demand by the State but sought by others other than the State, like from the people of the country, is not at the same level of demand because the State is the largest market and from it comes all funding for all things, making the little and the many the same. What the State funds becomes larger necessarily. Commoners, on the other hand, when they seek a *ṣinā`a*, their seeking is not general, and their market is not profitable. And God almighty has power over whatever He wills.

20. On the Relation Between the Condition of a Country and *Ṣanā'i`*

As a country approaches the state of ruin, *ṣanā'i`* will desert it. The reason for this is as we previously explained: *al-ṣanā'i`* become of high quality when there is a need for them, and their products and services are in high demand. When the conditions of a country (*al-miṣr*) are characterized by weakness and senility as a result of decreased urbanization (*`umrān*) and population (*sākin*), luxury in such a country would also decrease and its people would revert to limiting themselves to the necessities given their conditions. Consequently, *al-ṣanā'i`* that were connected to luxury conditions disappear because those employed in such *ṣanā'i`* can no longer make a living (*ma`āsh*) from them, so they change their professions. Alternatively, *al-ṣanā'i`* will die out with their deaths. In either case, the form and art of such *ṣanā'i`* will go away in their entireties including sculptors, painters, goldsmiths, calligraphers, copyists, and masters of similar *ṣanā'i`* focused on luxury, will all disappear. Such *ṣanā'i`* will continue to decrease until they go extinct. And God is the Creator, the Knowing, praised and exalted He be.

21. On the Arabs and *Ṣanā'i`*

The Arabs are the people most distant from *ṣanā'i`* because they are more firmly rooted in rural-living (*badw*) than in urban-living, which calls for and supports *ṣanā'i`* and its like. The non-Arabs (*`ajam*) who lived in the East and the Christian nations, remnants of the Roman Empire, are more involved in *ṣanā'i`* than other peoples because they are more firmly rooted in urban-living and furthest from rural-living and the inhabitants of rural regions.

Even camels, which enabled the Arabs to blend with the wilderness and become accustomed to rural-living (*badw*), do not exist at all in these non-Arab countries, nor do they have pastures suitable for feeding camels or sand suitable for their breeding.

For this reason, we find that the homelands of the Arabs and what they owned with the spread of Islam had few *ṣanā'i`* altogether, until it was imported from other regions. Observe the non-Arab (*`ajam*)[68] nations like China, India, the lands of the Turks, and the Christian nations, in all these nations, *ṣanā'i`* are abundant and other nations imported them from them.

The non-Arabs (*`ajam*) of *al-Maghrib*, the Berbers, too, like the Arabs in this respect; in that, they are firmly rooted in rural-living (*badāwa*) for many years. The absence of established countries (*amṣār*) in their region (*quṭr*) attests to this fact, as we said. As it were, *ṣanā'i`* in *al-Maghrib*, therefore, are few in number and are not well-established except the weaving of wool and the tanning and stitching of leather. And when they built cities, they improved these *ṣanā'i`* greatly because they concerned the public and since these—wool and leather—were the most common merchandise in their region, again, due to their rural living conditions (*badāwa*).

---

68 Although the word *`ajam* is often used to refer to non-Arabs, its meanings should be understood contextually. At times, it may be used to refer to foreignness, strangeness, difference, or lack of intellect.

In the east, on the other hand, *ṣanā'i`* became established since the rule of ancient nations including the Persians, the Nabataeans, the Copts, the Israelites, the Greeks, and the Romans for very long epochs. Thus, all aspects of urban living became established including *ṣanā'i`* as we have explained; and their forms and designs were never erased.

As to Yemen, Bahrain, Oman, and the Peninsula (*al-Jazira*), they were ruled by the Arab. But their rule was shared with other nations for thousands of years. These other nations founded countries and cities therein and they reached advanced levels of development of urbanization and luxury including the nations of `Ad and the Thamud, and the Amalekites and the Himyar after them; and then the Arab rulers of the Tababi`a, and the Adhwa. These many nations alternating in ruling these countries resulted in a prolonged rule that produced cities that imprinted a lifestyle (*ṣibgha*) and produced many *ṣanā'i`* that took deep roots that did not wear out with the fall of the State (*dawla*) as we explained. Instead, these *ṣanā'i`* continued to renew until now. Yemen became known for such specific *ṣanā'i`* like embroidering fabrics, stripping cloth, and finely woven garments and silks. And God shall inherit the Earth and whoever is upon it and He is the better heir.

22. On Acquired Abilities

Whoever acquires an ability in one *ṣināʿa* will be unlikely to master another. For example, a tailor who had acquired the habit of tailoring (*khiyāṭa*) and mastered it well and has its skills firmly rooted in his soul, will not afterwards master the art of carpentry (*nijāra*) or building (*bināʾ*) unless one does so when the first was not yet firmly established and its color (*ṣibgha*) not yet established. The reason for this is that abilities (*malakāt*) are descriptors and colors for the self (*nafs*). As such they cannot crowd at once. It is easier for a person who is still in the natural state, unformatted,[69] to accept abilities (*malakāt*) as he would be better prepared to acquire them. When the self (*nafs*) had been colored by another *malaka* and leaves its natural state (*fiṭra*), its readiness to master another *malaka* is weakened due to it being already colored by the acquired *malaka*, making its reception of another *malaka* even weaker. These facts are obvious and attested to in the real world. It is very rare to find some master of a *ṣināʿa* who perfects one, then moves on to perfect another, to the extent that he becomes equally good in both. Even scientists whose *malaka* is intellectual (*fikriyya*), still they are subject to this phenomenon. Whoever amongst scientists had acquired the *malaka* of one science and became good at is unlikely to master another science to the same degree of his mastery of the first. Instead, his mastery of the second, at best, will be limited. The cause for this phenomenon is found in what we have mentioned about the self's readiness and its color being colored by the first acquired *malaka* that had taken hold of the self. And God almighty knows more and by Him we succeed; no Lord but Him.

[69] The Arabic word used is *fiṭra*, which carries the connotation of "uninitiated." I have chosen the English word "formatted" due to its connotations of "formatting" a blank computer disk—a process which solidifies the type of computer on which one can use the disk, specializing it and thereby limiting its cross-specialty applications.

23. On the Hierarchy of *Ṣanā'i`*

One should know that human *ṣanā'i`* are numerous due to the fact that human works in city-living are many. In fact, they are too many to limit or enumerate. However, they can be classified based on what is necessary in urban living or noble by status. Therefore, we will detail these and leave out the rest.

From the category of necessary *ṣanā'i`*, we shall list agriculture (*filāḥa*), building (*binā'*), tailoring (*khiyāṭa*), carpentry (*nijāra*), and knitting (*ḥiyāka*). As to the noble *ṣanā'i`*, examples would include midwifery (*tawlīd*), writing (*kitāba*), printing (*wirāqa*), singing (*ghinā'*), and medicine (*ṭibb*).

Midwifery is necessary in urban-living (*`umrān*) and a public concern, for through it, life-birthing is made possible and assured and whose subjects are the born babies and the mothers.

Medicine, on the other hand, preserves the health of the human being and protects them against disease. It is a branch of natural sciences (*`ilm a-ṭabī`a*) and its subject is the human body.

The functions of writing and its derivatives like printing, including the memorializing of what humans need along with solutions thereto and their protection against forgetfulness, are as a messenger of human self-consciousness to those who are distant and absent, eternalizing results of ideas and sciences in books, and elevating the existence of meanings.

Singing is the range of graded tones of voices and the manifestation of their beauty to the listener. All these three *ṣanā'i`* are compelling enough to the extent that they will be present in the courts of the great kings and in their private circles, earning its masters honors not earned by masters of other *ṣanā'i`*.

Other *ṣanā'i`*, mostly likely, are derived and complementary to the above-mentioned ones, and they are different depending on the purposes and needs. And God knows best what is right.

24. On Agriculture

The product of this *ṣināʿa* is the extraction of foods (*aqwāt*) and grains through the preparation of the soil to sow it, the taking care of plants by irrigation and nurture until they mature; then the harvesting of the ears (*sunbul*) and the extraction of the grains out of their husks and the design of activities to achieve these tasks as well as the establishment of the causes and effects relevant to these processes.

Agriculture is the most ancient of all *ṣanāʾiʿ*, for it provides the food (*qūt*) that makes human life full and complete (*mukammil*), since the human being (*insān*) cannot exist without food. For this reason, this *ṣināʿa* was especially connected to rural-living, which, as we explained before, precedes urban-living and is older than it. As a result, this *ṣināʿa* has become a rural undertaking, not one undertaken by urban-dwellers, who do not get to know anything about it because their conditions are secondary to rural-living, making their *ṣanāʾiʿ* also secondary to the *ṣanāʾiʿ* of the rural people and dependent on them. And God almighty establishes people in whatever path He wishes.

25. On Building

Building (*bināʾ*) is the first of the *ṣanāʾiʿ* undertaken by the city-dwellers and the oldest. Building is the knowledge of work required to take houses and homes as places for shelter and rest for bodies in the cities. This is so because human beings are endowed with the ability to think about the outcomes of the circumstances of their living conditions. Therefore, human beings must think about the means to protect themselves against heat and cold, including devising houses with walls and roofs surrounding all sides. This ability to think (*jibilla*) makes human beings different in this regard. The difference in home-building is also determined by how temperate the climate is. Some would follow the practice of the people of zones one, two, three, four, five, or six. But rural dwellers, on the other hand, will not consider this at all, due to their ideas being limited to their own *ṣanāʾiʿ*, and not familiar with human *ṣanāʾiʿ*, resorting instead to life in holes and caves that are prepared without much treatment and improvements.

The temperate people who take houses for shelter become very numerous and have many houses in one flat area. They become strangers to each other and no longer know each other. They worry about being attacked in their homes, so they find it necessary to protect their community by surrounding it with a wall or a ditch full of water to guard them, which makes them a single city or a single country. Inside, they establish governing authorities that would defend some against some. For protection, they build fortresses and castles for themselves and for the people under their charge. These would be like kings, princes, or tribal chiefs.

Building in cities is different. In each city, a building will depend on its inhabitants' conventions, familiarity; and on their preferences, likes and dislikes; and on the difference in their economic status such as poverty and riches. In addition to the differences that distinguish among cities, there are also differences among the people of the same city.

Some would take as home castles and greatly constructed spaces consisting of a number of dwellings and houses with many rooms reflecting the number of children, workers, and family members. Such homes will be constructed from stone joined together with quicklime coated with paint and plaster. They would exceed limits to furnish and decorate everything in order to show how much care they devote to their homestead.

Additionally, they prepare cellars and underground holes (*maṭāmīr,* sing. *maṭmūr*) for the storage of their food. They also establish stables for tying up their transport animals if they owned an army or if they have large entourage of servants and associates, like princes and other people of similar status.

Some among them build a small home or house for themselves and for their children to live in. They seek nothing beyond that because their condition does not support doing so. They would rely instead on natural shelters for human protection against the elements, which varies due to innumerable climate variations contained between the two described extremes.

This *ṣinā`a* is also needed when kings and rulers of states found huge cities with high structures (*hayākil*). They are exceedingly meticulous when devising plans and raising bodies with technical perfection, whose effects feed back into further developing the *ṣinā`a* allowing it to reach high level of development. Therefore, the *ṣinā`a* of building stimulates interest in such activities everywhere. However, interest is highest in moderate zones, the fourth zone and the zones adjacent to it on either side. In zones that are intemperate, however, there is no building activity. Instead, people living in those zones take for home enclosures made of reeds and clay or take shelter in caves and holes.

People involved in this *ṣinā`a* are of different skill levels: Some are skilled and imaginative and some lack such skills and traits. The *ṣinā`a* itself varies, encompassing many types: building with preformed stones or with bricks (*ajūr*) to erect walls by gluing the stones or bricks with each other by clay and quicklime, which fuse together, turning the parts into one structure as if it were one piece.

Building can also be accomplished using pure soil (*turāb*). To build a wall, they would take two wooden boards, conventionally measured so as to preserve a standard within the region. The average size is four-by-two cubits (*dhirā`*). The boards are placed on the foundation. They would be proportionally separated by a distance dependent on the width of the foundation the builder considers appropriate. The boards will be joined together with wooden connectors held together with ropes or fasteners. The two remaining sides of the empty space between the two boards are sealed by two other small boards. The spaces created by this structure is then filled with soil (*turāb*) mixed with quicklime mixture that is pounded with special mixers used for such a purpose, smoothing everything and mixing it thoroughly with quicklime. Soil is gradually added, twice and thrice until the empty void between the two boards is filled with the mixture of soil and quicklime, which becomes a single body. The process is repeated, replacing the two boards next and on top of each block until the wall stands cemented together as if it were a single piece. Such a wall structure will be then called *ṭābiya* and its maker is called *ṭawwāb*.

Among the *ṣanā'i`* of building is the covering of walls with quicklime, which is first dissolved with water and allowed to ferment for a week or two depending on the average time needed, depending on its composition and the environment that preserves its integrity and resistance to heat, which can prevent fusion and adherence of particles of the mixture. Once the desired mixture is attained, it is poured down from the top of the wall to the foundation, connecting all parts of the wall.

The *ṣanā'i`* of building also includes roof works. Wooden beams that are of carpentry or standard qualities are placed across the two walls of the house. On top of these beams, wooden boards are nailed down before a mixture of soil and quicklime (*kils*) is poured down on top of the wooden surface. The mixture is spread with a special tool that mixes and combines the various elements of the mixture, enabling it to adhere together. The platform is then resurfaced with quicklime sheet the same way the walls were surfaced.

The *ṣanāʾiʿ* of building includes decoration and ornamentation works. Shapes formed from gypsum are placed upon the walls. The gypsum is mixed with water, and then solidified again, with some moisture still in it. Symmetrical figures and patterns are chiseled out of it with iron tools, until it looks fascinating and congenial. The walls could be covered with pieces of marble, brick, clay, shells, or jet. The material may be divided either into similar- or contrasting-shaped parts. These pieces are arranged in whatever patterns and arrangements that can be observed from distance, making the wall appear like a carefully arranged garden.

Building involves other things like the construction of waterholes and cisterns for running water to the homes where marble containers and bottles are carefully prepared. They have orifices in the middle to permit the water of the cistern to flow out. The water comes to the cistern from the outside through conduits bringing it into the houses. These and other activities are part of building (*bināʾ*).

The *ṣanāʾiʿ* are distinguished from one another by the skills and imaginations of the persons involved in them. Urban dwelling increases and spreads in the city, resulting in an increase in the number of builders. Oftentimes, rulers consult expert builders. Their opinion is needed because in crowded cities, people compete for everything including space and air, high and low, wanting to take advantage of everything including the appearance and architecture of buildings, which can damage the walls.

Such competition drives people to deny their neighbors anything except that which is covered by an explicit right. People often dispute roadways, easements, and access to running water, and waste channels. Other disputes may arise when someone claims someone else's right of use, complains about a shared wall or its height, or the water cannel in dense neighborhoods. In other instances, a neighbor may raise a claim against another, accusing him of causing damage to his wall, seeking an order to destroy the wall and pay damages to the owner or to anyone who might end up owning it in cases of partnership; all this to prevent property loss or future profit losses, and other similar cases.

All these matters are clear only to those who are experts in building, who can study the joints, weight centers, support beams, wall tilt and uprightness; types of buildings, rates of water flow in pipes and open channels, making sure that these waterways do not damage the home and its walls, etc. These experts have the necessary knowledge and skills that others do not have—notwithstanding the fact that these experts, too, differ in terms of the perfection, or lack thereof, of skill depending on the state of the country and its power.

We have presented that *ṣanā'i`* and their perfection are connected to the perfection of city-dwelling and the plurality of *ṣanā'i`* is connected to the number of those demanding it. Therefore, if the State is rural, in its early stage, it will lack interest in building to the benefit of other regions. This was the case with al-Walid Ibn Abd al-Malik when he decided on building the Madina Mosque, Quds Mosque, and his prayer hall in the Levant (*Sham*). He sent to the King of Rome in Constantinople requesting working experts in building. The king sent him enough men to build these mosques as he had planned them. Masters of such *ṣinā`a* know about relevant engineering including building erect walls using the plumb, flowing water through gravity by raising the source, and similar things that require expertise in specific matters. They also must know how to move heavy loads with the help of pulleys.

Huge structures that are built using large stones cannot be lifted into place on a wall by the unaided strength of workmen alone. Therefore, the expert would contrive to multiply the force of the rope by passing it through holes, constructed according to geometrical proportions, which facilitate the lifting of heavy objects. Such a pulley system, carefully engineered, allowed for the lifting of heavy objects with little human effort. These methods are well-known and shared among peoples. It was used to build the structures that are still standing and believed to have been built during the time before Islam (*jāhiliyya*)—leading some to assume that it was built by people whose bodies were of a size corresponding to that of the structures. This is not so. Rather, it was accomplished through engineering innovations, as we have mentioned. This, you must understand. And God, almighty, creates whatever He wishes.

26. On Carpentry

This *ṣināʿa* is one of the necessities of city dwelling. Its material is wood. God made in every created thing something useful that complements the necessities of the descendants of Adam (*ādamiyy;* human). One such a thing is trees. The trees provide humans with innumerable benefits known to everyone. One of the benefits of trees is their use as wood when they are dry. The first use of wood is as firewood to support their living. Dry wood can be used as sticks for support, protection, and other necessities; and as supports for loads that might tilt. Then, after that, trees have other uses for both urban and rural dwellers.

Rural dwellers use trees to make tent poles and pegs, for camel litters, and for lances, bows, and arrows for their weapons.

Urban dwellers use wood from trees for the roofs of their houses, for the locks of their doors, and for the chairs they sit on. Each of these things depends on wood as raw material. However, it cannot be made into what it is without the *ṣināʿa.* The *ṣināʿa* dedicated to each functional tool determines its form; however, carpentry is basic in all different levels and aims of using wood.

The master of this *ṣināʿa,* the carpenter, must first split the wood into smaller pieces or into boards. Then, these pieces are put together in the required form. In doing so, the carpenter attempts with his skills to prepare these pieces by the proper arrangement, making them elements of the particular shape. Carpentry is a profession that is necessary for urban dwelling.

Then, when urban-dwelling increases, increasing luxury, people would compete in making these objects like wooden ceilings, doors, chairs, or bowls unique and more elegant; these things come to be produced in a most elegant way through mastery of strange techniques—techniques that are complementary and in no way necessary. Such techniques would include, for example, the carvings on doors and chairs, the preparations of pieces in odd shapes, and their connecting together in calculated manner and nailing them together, so that they appear to the eye to be one piece whose difference and variance is harmonized by the symmetry of the final product. This added work is done in every object made from wood, turning it into very elegant things. The same applies to all wooden tools (*ālāt*) of whatever kind.

Carpentry is also needed for the construction of sea-crafts, which are made of boards and nails, geometric shapes modeled in the form of a large fish (*ḥūt*), imitating the way the fish swims in the water with its fins and belly. The shape is intended to make it easier for the ship to make contact with and cut through the water. For movement, instead of the animal motion that the fish does to move, the sea-craft is moved by the winds. It is often supported by the movement of oars, as is the case in naval fleets.

Fundamentally, this *ṣinā`a*, in all its forms, is rooted in engineering because producing the form from being a concept to an object requires knowing relative calculations, generally or specifically, and proportionality is the domain of engineering.

For this reason, the leading Greek engineers were all master carpenters. Euclid, the author of *the Book of the Principles of Engineering*, was a carpenter and was known as such. The same with Apollonius, the author of the book on Conics, and Menelaus, and others.

It is said that the first human to teach this *ṣinā`a* was Noah. With it, he constructed the ship of salvation, his prophetical miracle, during the Flood. In this story, it is possible that he was a carpenter. However, there is no reliable proof upon which we can build that he was the first to learn and/or teach carpentry, for it is too far in the past. The meaning of the story, and God knows best, is to indicate how ancient or old carpentry is since there was no story about it before the story of Noah, peace be upon him. So, he was made to appear as the first to learn it. So do learn the secrets of *ṣanā'i`* among human beings. And God, the Almighty, knows more, and through Him, one succeeds.

27. On the *Ṣinā`a* of Weaving and Tailoring

Know that people who are temperate, in the sense of humidity, must give some thought to warmth the same way they give thought to being. Warmth is obtained by rendering woven material protective against heat and cold. For this, yarn must be fused together, making it into single piece of cloth. The processes of fusing are weaving (*nasj*) and spinning (*ḥiyāka*).

Rural dwellers will be limited to weaving and spinning. Urban dwellers, on the other hand, would cut the cloth into smaller pieces and design it in a way that traces the human body fitting all around it and all around the body parts and shapes. The different pieces are then connected together with thread, until it becomes a single garment that fits the body and would be worn. The *ṣinā`a* that accomplish this altering is tailoring (*khiyāṭa*).

These two *ṣanā'i`* are necessary in city-living for human beings seeking comfort (*rafh*).

The first is for the purpose of weaving (*nasj*) the yarn (*ghazl*), which is from wool (*ṣūf*), cashmere[70] (*kittān*), and cotton (*qutn*)—to generate length, propagate width, and strengthen the weaving; producing measured pieces including outerwear (*aksiya*) from wool due to its size, and clothes from cashmere and cotton for daily wear[71] (*libās*).

The second *ṣinā`a* is for designing the weaved/woven materials to fit different human forms and different traditions and tastes.

The material is first cut with scissors into pieces that fit the limbs of the body; the pieces are then connected together skillfully

[70] While *kittān* translates from Arabic as "cashmere," the same word *kittān* may, in Berber dialects, refer to cloth more generally.

[71] The converse of outerwear, these are clothes that go beneath outerwear and range from undergarments to shorts.

using thread, bands, quilting, or cutting openings depending on the type of *ṣinā`a*.

This *ṣinā`a* is the specialty of city dwellers not because rural dwellers can dispense with it. Rather, because they use the full woven cloth as cover that they wrap themselves with. Therefore, designing clothes, through precise measurement, cuts, fitting, and sewing of the material, is the art and practice (*madhhab*) of urban dwellers.

Understanding this would reveal the wisdom behind the prohibition of wearing sewn garments while on the Hajj journey. The validity of Hajj is dependent upon giving up connections to worldly matters, all of it, and returning to God almighty in the form He created humans at the beginning. This would prevent the worshipper's heart from being attached to any of the practices of luxury and indulgence: no cologne/perfume, not women,[72] no woven clothes, no sewn shoes; no hunting or any other habit or practice that had colored one's self (*nafs*) and character (*khuluq*)—though he would necessarily lose all that with death. However, during Hajj, the human being comes as if they are coming to the day of resurrection full-heartedly and faithful to his Lord. One's reward, should they achieve such sincerity, will be that they will shed their sins and regain their state as to when their mother gave birth to them. Acknowledged (*subḥānak*) be You for how kind You are to Your worshippers and how compassionate You are with them in their search for guidance toward You!

These two *ṣanā'i`* are very ancient in the created world, because warmth is necessary for humans who live in cities in temperate zones. As to those who live off the temperate zones, they do not need to keep warm. For this reason, we hear that the people who

---

[72] The case ending on the Arabic word is creates some confusion here for the translator. Ibn Khadun might be saying "no women" or "except for women." He may also have intended to say both, since on the one hand, women, unlike men, can wear woven materials; but since he is making the point that during hajj, person is supposed to disassociate themselves from all connections to worldly things and pleasures, he might be also saying that there can be no companionship with women during hajj.

live in the first zone of the region of Sudan are naked most of the time.

As to the origins of these *ṣanā'i`*, the common view is that they originated with Idris, who is the most ancient of prophets. They are also often attributed to Ḥermes and some think that Hermes is Idris. And God, *subḥānahu*, is the Creator, the Knowing.

28. On Midwifery

Tawlīd is the *ṣinā`a* referring to the extracting of the to-be-born human from their mother's belly including the instance of pulling them gently out of the womb and the preparation work that led to that moment. It also includes the caring for the baby after it is born, as we shall mention.

The *ṣinā`a* is, generally, the specialty of women, since the private parts of women may be exposed to other women only. The woman who does this is called *qābila* (midwife), the term is borrowed from the literal sense which implies giving and accepting, in that the woman in labor in a way gives the embryo to the midwife, and the latter accepts it (*taqbaluh*).

This is so because when the creation of the embryo is completed in the womb; it went through all the stages therein, reached the end of its term and the number of days God allocated to it, which is about nine months in most cases, it seeks to exit driven by the instinct that God implanted in them. However, the opening is too tight and exiting becomes difficult (*ya`sur*) to the extent that it may rip some of the sides of the vagina due to pressure, or cause detachment of membranes connecting the uterus to the womb. All this is painful and results in increased hurt, which is the meaning of "*talaq;*" whereby the *qābila* becomes a helper in that, to some extent, massaging the back, the thighs and the areas near the womb. She, thus, simulates the pushing (*dafa`a*) of the embryo out, and facilitates the difficulties encountered in this connection as much as she can, aided by her experience dealing with this hardship.

When the embryo has come out, there remains between it and the womb a connector through which it was fed, through the umbilical cord to its stomach. That cord is an unessential body part exclusively needed for feeding the child. Therefore, the midwife cuts it but in a way that she does not go beyond the place where it becomes extra and does not harm the stomach of the child or the womb of the mother. She then treats the cut area with cauterization or by whatever other treatment of cut-healing she sees fit.

Additionally, when the embryo comes out of that narrow opening with its soft bones that can easily be bent and curved, it may happen that the forms and shapes of its body parts change, given how recent the birth is to the time of growth and formation. The midwife, then, massages and adjusts every organ and body part until it has resumed its natural shape and its predetermined state, making its creation complete. After that, she goes back to the woman in labor (*nafsa'*) and massages and kneads her, so that whatever membranes of the embryo still inside her may come out. Such membranes may be late in coming out. On such an occasion, it is feared that the constricting tissues might contract and assume its natural position before all the membranes, which are extra, are pushed out. They might become putrid, which might spread to the womb causing death. The midwife takes precautions against such a scenario by helping with the push to flush out all membranes whose exit might have been delayed.

She then returns to the newborn (*mawlūd*). She anoints its body parts with oils and drying medicine to strengthen it and to dry up the fluids of the womb. She attends to its jaws to allow it to breathe better. She stimulates its nose to cause it to sneeze, which empties its brain cavities. She makes it gargle using an electuary, in order to prevent its bowels from becoming obstructed or its walls struck together.

Then, she treats the woman in labor for the weakness caused by the labor pains and the pain that the separation causes her womb (*raḥim*). For although the newborn was not an attached organ of the pregnant woman, nonetheless, its development inside the womb made it attached to the body of the mother, just like an attached body part is, which explains the pain that accompanies the separation, which resembles the pain of cutting. Given that, the midwife would then attend to the pain felt in the vagina, resulting from tear wounds caused by the pressure of pushing out the newborn. We find that midwives are best prepared to cure all these ills and traumas associated with birth. They are better prepared to deal with any ills that may inflict a newborn during the suckling period than any skilled doctor, from birth until they are weaned. This is so because the human body, at this stage, is a human body due to the force of nature only. However, after the child is weaned, it becomes a human body by lived experience, which increases their need for the services of a medical doctor henceforth.

As you can see, this *ṣinā`a* is necessary for the humankind to endure due to the nature of humankind, whereas the existence of individuals would not be complete without it in most cases. Other individuals may not depend on midwifery due to them being created through divine intervention, God's miracle and break from the normal. Examples of divine intervention at birth include the case of God's prophets, may God's blessings and prayers be with them. Other cases of divine intervention birth include divine inspiration and guidance instilled in the newborn making their existence independent of this *ṣinā`a*.

As to miraculous birth, that happened many times. It has, thus, been reported that the Prophet Muhammad was born with the umbilical cord cut, circumcised, and with his hands placed upon the earth and gazing heavenwardly. Jesus' birth was the same—in the cradle and other things.

Inspirational birth (*ilhām*), too, cannot be denied. If non-speaking animals (*al-ḥayawānāt al-`ujum*), such as bees for example, have enjoyed the strangest of inspirations, why should one not assume the same for the human being who is favored over animals, and especially those humans privileged by God's providence?

Furthermore, the common instinct of newborn children that causes them to seek their mother's breast is clear evidence of the existence of an inspiration-based ability (*ilhām `āmm*) in them. Matters of divine care are too great to be grasped completely.

From this, the incorrectness of the opinion of al-Farabi and other Andalusian philosophers can be understood. They argued against the occurrence of extinction (*inqirāḍ*) of species and the impossibility of interruption (*inqiṭā`*) of living beings, especially related to the human species. They said: If individual human beings were to be interrupted, the existence of midwifery would be impossible, for the existence of such *ṣinā`a* is dependent upon the existence of midwifery, which is necessary for the existence of the human species. For even if we were to assume that a child would be born without the help of this *ṣinā`a*, and without being taken care of by this *ṣinā`a* until it was weaned, still, its continued existence (*baqā'*) would not be possible. The existence of *ṣanā'i`* without the abstract thinking (*fikr*) is impossible because *ṣanā'i`* are the fruits of thinking and they are connected to abstract thought.

Avicenna undertook the refutation of this opinion, because he was opposed to it and because he held that interruption in certain species is a possibility and that the created world could end (*kharāb*) and restart anew. He claims that, for cosmological forces and strange phenomenon that repeat over epochs of time, they require the fermentation of clay appropriate to his[73] temperament with the help of appropriate heat to produce the human being. Then, an animal is configured with the inspiration to care and love it until it is complete and ready for separation. Avicenna explained this carefully in a treatise he called *The Treatise of Hayy Ibn Yaqzan.*

This reasoning is not correct—although I agree with him in regard to the end of species, for other reasons than what he relied on to reach the same conclusion. His evidence is built on relating events to the necessary cause—necessary in that the outcome is certain. The theory of the select agency (*fā`il mukhtār*) is a proof against him for there is no connection between claiming the select agency and between events and perpetual power (*qudra qadīma*) and there is no need for making such a connection.

Even if we were to accept such connection for the sake of argument, the extent of the application of such theory is that the existence of such an individual will be connected to inspiration

---

[73] The human being's

(*ilhām*) for its presence in non-speaking animals. In such a case, one must ask, still, what is the necessity that requires that? If inspiration (*ilham*) is created in non-speaking animals, what would prevent its creation in the newborn of the same kind (*nafsih*), as we described above?

The creation of inspiration (*ilhām*) in an individual (*shakhṣ*) for one's own benefit makes more sense than creating inspiration in one an individual for the benefit of someone else—the two theories, that of al-Farabi and that of Avicenna, bore evidence for their own incorrectness in their particular approaches, as I have established. And God knows more.

29. On Medicine

The *ṣināʿa* of medicine (*al-ṭibb*) is needed in cities and countries and not in rural areas. It is necessary in cities and settled countries given the widely known benefits of such a *ṣināʿa*. The mission of it is the preservation of health among those who are healthy, and the repulsion of illness among those who are ill using medical treatment so that they are cured of their diseases.

It should be known that the origin of all illnesses is in foods (*aghdhiya*), as stated by the Prophet Muhammad, may God's peace and blessing be with him: "The stomach is the locus of disease; dieting is the chief treatment; and the origin of every disease is indigestion."

The meaning of "the stomach is the locus of disease" is obvious (*ẓāhir*).

As for the statement, "Dieting is the chief treatment," the word "*ḥimya*" refers to hunger—which is, in a sense, protection against food. It follows, then, that hunger is the greatest medicine, the origin of all medicines. As for the statement, "the origin of every disease is indigestion," the meaning of "*al-barda*" is the introduction of new food to the food already in the stomach before it has been digested.

The explanation of this statement is this: God created the human being (*al-insān*). God preserved life of the human being by food. The human being would consume the food by eating it; then flood it with digestive and extractive forces until it becomes fluid-blood suitable for consumption by the various parts of the body, be it flesh or bones. The fluid nutrients are then picked up by the growth cells, which transform it into flesh and bones.

Digestion (*haḍm*), then, means the boiling of food using the instinctive heat (*al-ḥarāra al-gharīziyya*), one step after another, until the food becomes, literally, part of the body. In other words, when the food enters the mouth, it is masticated by the jaws. After that, the heat of the mouth will affect it, boiling it slightly and converting its structure a bit. This can be observed when a morsel of food is taken and chewed well; its taste will be different from when it was a morsel when it first enters the mouth.

The same happens in the stomach: The heat of the stomach cooks it until it becomes chyme (*kaymus*), which is the extract of the boiled food (*maṭbūkh*), which is sent to the liver; the remaining residue in the bowels will be sent out through the two orifices.

The heat of the liver, then, cooks down the chyme, until it becomes fresh blood (*daman `abīṭan*) that is covered by a foam, which is the yellow bile (*al-ṣafrā'*). Some dry parts, known as the black bile residue (*al-sawdā'*), would settle. The coarse parts, known as the phlegm (*al-balgham*) are not sufficiently cooked by these natural acids (*al-ḥarr al-gharīzī*). The liver then sends all of it into the veins and arteries. There, the natural enzymes (*al-hāl al-gharīzī*) start to cook them—turning them into pure blood, which converts into hot and humid steam that sustains the animal spirit (*al-rūḥ al-ḥayawānī*), and from which the growth cells would pick its fill, turning it into flesh, and its coarse parts into bones. Then, the body excretes the excesses that are not needed in the form of different particles including sweat, saliva, mucus, and tears. This is the form of nutrients and their transformation from energy (*quwwa*) into events in the form of generated flesh. It should be clear then that the origin of diseases, or most of the diseases, is fevers (*al-ḥummiyyāt*). The cause of it is that natural acid (*al-ḥarr al-gharīzī*) may fail to finish cooking in every stage of the digestive track, causing some of the food to remain uncooked. This in turn can be caused by excess food in the stomach that would overwhelm the natural acid. Or it could be caused by adding more food in the stomach before it is able to finish cooking the food already there. In this case, the natural acid would busy itself in cooking the new arrival, leaving the first food uncooked. Or the natural acid may spread itself thin cooking both foods at the same time, failing to cook parts of both. The stomach would, nonetheless, pass the food in such a condition, making the heat of the liver incapable of cooking it, too. It is possible that some unprocessed food remains in the liver. Yet, the liver would pass all, including the unprocessed food, to the veins as is. When the body has extracted its needs, it sends the excess along with other leftovers in the form of excreted sweat, tears, and saliva, if it can. However, the body may fail to clear all of it, leaving some in the veins, liver, and stomach; this accumulation would increase over time.

Since every humid substance that is not cooked and processed would rot, the rotten food would contaminate other unprocessed food; and this is called mixture (*al-khild*). All rotten foods would generate strange heat, and when it occurs in the human body, it will be called fever (*al-ḥummā*).

One can experiment with this by leaving food out until it becomes rotten. It is the same phenomenon with animal dung, and how it emits heat and how it takes its course.

This is the meaning of fevers (*al-ḥummiyyāt*) in the human body, which is the chief disease and the origins of all of them as explained in the tradition (Hadith).

The treatment of fevers consists of cutting off food from the ill person for a determined number of weeks and eating only appropriate foods until he heals.

In the case of good health, the same procedure (fasting) serves as a preventive treatment for this and other illnesses and the reference for this is in the Hadith.

In some cases, the food contamination could affect a specific organ. In this case, the organ might become ill, causing injuries to the body localized in the main organs or other organs. When an organ is diseased, its disease may transfer to effect energies that it enables. This summarizes all the diseases (*amrāḍ*). And the origins of these diseases, generally, are found in foods and the knowledge of all these matters is with the medical doctor (*al-ṭabīb*).

These diseases are more likely to strike city and country dwellers because of the abundance of foods, the diversity in their living ways, their lack of reliance on a single kind of food, and the absence of set times for meals. These people, urban dwellers, often mix their meals to include spices, vegetables, and fruits—dry and moist—when they process and cook their meals. They do not limit themselves to one or a few types. We have documented cases in which the cooked meals of just one day consisted of forty types including plant and animal, making for a very strange temper. It is possible that it is too strange to agree with the body and its organs and parts.

Moreover, the air in cities becomes foul due to its contact with rotten steam rising from the large amounts of trash. This is important because the air energizes the spirits (*munashshita li-'l-arwāḥ*) and such energy strengthens the natural acids and enzymes needed for digestion.

Furthermore, sporting activities are missing in city living, for city dwellers are sedentary; thereby exercising does not take anything from them and leaves no effects on them. Consequently, the occurrence of illness is frequent in the city and urban regions, making their need to this *ṣinā`a* (medicine) proportional to the rate of illness and sickness.

Whereas people who live in rural areas and whose foods are generally little, and who are likely to go hungry due to the scarcity of grains (*al-ḥubūb*); they become accustomed to hunger to the extent some would think that it is an acquired trait because of how persistent it is amongst them. Spices are few or non-existent. Therefore, cooking using herbs and fruits would require the luxury of city-living, from which they are disconnected. Instead, they eat simple meals, removed from other mixes, and make its temper closer to matching the temper of the body (*al-badan*).

The air in which rural dwellers live, too, is less contaminated due to limited steam and foulness associated with living closely to each other. Or rural dwellers live may live in different air all together when they live apart from each other or move around.

Sports (*al-riyāḍa*) are common among rural dwellers because of their frequent movements riding horses, hunting, or doing any other task. These exercising activities aid in digestion and improve the breakdown of eaten foods. Adding one food to another in the stomach also would not occur, which would enhance their temper and protect them from diseases—making their need for medicine limited. As a result, medical doctors do not exist in the countryside, as a general observation. The non-existence of medical doctors is due to the lack of need: Were medical doctors needed, they would have existed, because the doctor would be able to make a living in the countryside and thus reside there; but that is not the case. "Thus is God's *Sunna* (System) among his created people; and one cannot find an alternative to God's *Sunna*."

30. On Calligraphy and Writing

It should be known that that calligraphy and writing are among the *ṣanā'i`* developed by humans. This includes drawings and shapes of letters connoting the audible words that indicate what is on the mind of the self (*al-nafs*). It comes second in the linguistic skillsets, and it is a noble undertaking, since it is one of the special abilities of humans that distinguishes them from animals.

Additionally, it reveals what is on one's mind, transfers information across borders to distant lands, delivers messages on needs, and allows those who specialize in this *ṣinā`a* to earn an income. It also enables people to access the sciences, knowledge, and the writings of those who wrote down their discoveries and history. Therefore, due to these functions and benefits, it is regarded as a noble *ṣinā`a*.

Humans upgrade their potential for such skills into practice through learning and the degree of such skills is proportional to the level of social interaction and level of urban development, which increase demand for luxury and for such skills. Therefore, good quality of writing in the city is more prevalent, as is the case with the abundance of many *ṣanā'i`*.

We have already stated that the existence of many *ṣanā'i`* is more likely among urban dwellers and in city-living environments. In this case, too, we find most of the rural dwellers being illiterate, unable to read and write, and if some of them are able to read and write their writing is basic and their reading is superficial.

Learning calligraphy in countries whose urbanization exceeds the limits is finer, better, and easier than learning it in less dense urban areas; because the ṣinā`a has taken hold in such an environment.

We received reports that in contemporary Egypt (*Miṣr*), there are teachers specializing in calligraphy, instructing students with rules and guidelines about writing each letter; in addition to teaching them about the abstract knowledge related to the use of letters and words. This level of specialization enables the learner to increase their engagement with the science, enhance their handle of the learned content, and perfect their capacity. This is consistent with the general rule that the abundance and perfection of *ṣanā'i`* is connected to the level of urbanization and the density of city-living. The same applies to the Arabic written word.

Arabic writing had already reached its most developed, accurate, and excellent stage in the Tababi`a dynasty, because, there, urban and luxury living reached its zenith. The writing system there became known as *al-khaṭṭ al-ḥumayrī* (Himyarite script). It was transferred from there to al-Hirah, because the dynasty of the clan of al-Mundhir was there. They were related to the Tubabi`a, and were in solidarity with them. They re-instated the rule of the Arabs in Iraq. Writing among them was not as good as it was among the Tubabi`a, given the separation between the two states (*dawlatayn*). And this was reflected in the limitedness of urbanization and its effects, including the abundance and *ṣanā'i`*. From al-Hirah, the people of al-Ta'if and Quraysh learned writing, according to some reports. The person who learned the art of writing from al-Hirah is Sufyan Ibn Umayya, and some say Harb Ibn Umayya, who learned it from Aslam Ibn Sudra. This is a more possible opinion than the one that suggested that they learned it from the clan of Iyad of the Iraqi people, based on the poem of one of their own who said:

> *A people to whom belongs the area of the Iraq, who,*
>
> *when they march, they march with written word*
>
> *(khaṭṭ) and the pen (qalam).*

This is an unlikely theory because, even if Iyad settled in the area of Iraq, they maintained their rural-living way of life. Writing is one of the *ṣanā'i`* that is common in urban living. The meaning of the verse of the poet is that Iyad were closer to writing and the pen than other Arabs, because they were closer to urban environments.

I became familiar with the idea that the people of Hijaz learned writing from the people of al-Hira, who had learned it from the Tababi`a (Tubba`) and Himyar. Such an idea is the most plausible one. It is referenced in the book *al-Takmila* by Ibn al-Abbar when he introduced Ibn Farrukh al-Qayrawani al-Qasi al-Andalusi, a companion of Malik, may God be pleased with him; he is `Abdullah Ibn Farrukh Abd al-Rahman Ibn Ziyid Ibn An`am. On the authority of his father, he said:

> "I said to Abdallah Ibn Abbas: 'People Quraysh, tell me about this Arabic book (*kitab*). Did you use to write it before God sent Muhammad, may God's peace and blessings be with him? Did you use to connect the connecting letters and isolate the non-connecting letters like the *alif, lam, mim,* and *nun*?' He replied: 'Yes.' I continued: 'From whom did you learn it?' He replied: 'From Harb Ibn Umayya.' I asked: 'and from whom did Harb learn it?' He replied: 'From Abdallah Ibn Jad`an.' I asked: 'And from whom did Abdallah Ibn Jad`an learn it?' He replied: 'From the people of al-Anbar.' I asked: 'And from whom did the people of al-Anbar learn it?' He replied: 'From a visitor from Yemen.' I asked: 'And from whom did the visitor learn it?' He replied: 'From al-Khilljan Ibn al-Qasam, the scribe who wrote down the revelation to the prophet Hood, peace be with him. It is he who said:
>
> Is it every year, that you update it,
>
> And an opinion that is to be explained in a different way?
>
> And death is better than a life of which we are made to be ashamed,

In it Jurhum, among the made-ashamed,
and the Himyar.'

End of quote from the *Kitab al-Takmila*, as reported by Ibn al-Abari; at whose end he added: "I was told this by Abu Bakr Ibn Abi Himayara in his book, on the authority of Abu Bahr Ibn al-'As, on the authority of Abu al-Walid al-Waqshi, on the authority of Abu Umar al-Tala`anki Ibn Abu Abdallah Ibn Mufrij. From his written notes I referenced it on the authority of Abu Sa`id Ibn Yunus, on the authority of Muhammad Ibn Musa Ibn al-Nu`man, on the authority of Yahya Ibn Muhammad Ibn Hashish Ibn Umar Ibn Ayyub al-maghafiri al-Tunsi, on the authority of Bahlul Ibn Ubayda al-Himyi on the authority of Abdullah Ibn Farrukh. End."

In Himyar, there was a script called al-Musnad, whose letters were written separately. Learning it was prohibited without their permission. The people of al-Mudar learned writing Arabic from Himyar. However, they did not write it well, as is the case with *ṣanā'ī`* that are practiced in rural areas. The *ṣanā'ī`*, when practiced in rural areas, are not firmly established in terms of methods and quality, lacking accuracy and elegance. Given the wide gap between rural dwellers and *ṣinā`a*, which they can do without in most cases (*fi al-akthar*), writing by the Arabs, then, was as primitive as their writing at this time—or close to it. Perhaps, we should say that the writing by the Arabs at this time shows a better technique, because of their proximity to urban areas and because of their interaction with other countries (*amṣār*) and nation-states (*duwal*). Mudar was more firmly rooted in rural-living and more remote from urban areas than the peoples of Yemen, Iraq, Syria, and Egypt. Consequently, at the beginning of Islam, written Arabic was not of the best quality nor of the greatest accuracy and excellence. It was not even of average quality, since the Arabs' place of living was in the desert and wilderness and they were removed from *ṣanā'ī`*. This state of the written word was the cause of what happened to the writing of the Muṣḥaf, as it can be observed. The Companions wrote it down by hand and such handwriting was not systematized. And since systemic writing is what insures its quality, their written notes conflicted with the requirements and rules of the written forms as developed by the masters of the written word.

People who followed the first generation of Authoritative ancestors (Salaf and Tabi`un) adopted the style of writing from the Companions (*Sahaba*) of the Prophet—the best among God's creation, and wrote down God's revelation—His Book and His Word. The Tabi`un's adoption of the Companions' style was to honor them and to seek their grace; the same way scribes would adopt (*iqtafā*) the writings of a saint or a scholar for the sake of grace, by following the style and form of their writing, be it correct or incorrect. Scholars have later referenced the Companions' writings and identified the incorrect content by adding a note over it in the exact location, to alert readers to it. Therefore, you should not give credence to the claims by some fools who contended that the Companions were experts in the *ṣinā`a* of writing (*khaṭṭ*) and that what is assumed to be a mistake in their writings (*khuṭūṭihim*) and a violation of the principles of writing is not so; but it is just another way of doing it.

For example, they would argue that the addition of the *alif* in the phrase "*lā adhbaḥannahu*" is a warning that the slaughter did not take place. Or, in another example, they argue the addition of the letter "*yā*'" in "*bi'ay-ayd*" as being a note about the completeness of divine power. And many other examples like these about errors that reflect the Companions' lack of full and complete control of the writing system during their time.

These fools would make such claims only thinking that they are absolving (*tanzīh*) the Companions of shortcomings in relations to their writing abilities (*ijādat al-khaṭṭ*). They thought that being able to write is a matter of perfection and they wanted to absolve them of any imperfection by claiming that they are perfect in writing and justified what is a simple error in writing—and that is not good. It should be known that writing is not related to their perfection, for perfection is one of the urban *ṣanā'i`* that allow one to earn a living as indicated above.

Perfection in a *ṣinā`a* is an added value (*iḍāfī*)—not an absolute perfection. As such, imperfection (*nuqsān*) does have any effect on the self, be it in relation to religious or companionship matters. Rather, it impacts one's ability to make a living, which is also dependent on urbanization and collaboration, since writing indicates what is on the mind of people.

The Prophet, peace and blessing be with him, was illiterate and illiteracy here was perfection as it related to him given his standing (his station), his nobility, and his freedom from practical *ṣanā'i`*, which are all systems of building wealth and building cities.

On the other hand, illiteracy is not a perfection for us, for he, the Prophet, is dedicated to the service of his Lord while we are bound to collaborate on all worldly matters, which is the function of all *ṣanā'i`*, including abstract sciences. Therefore, the Prophet's perfection was attained despite his illiteracy, unlike us; in fact, his was disinterest in the *ṣinā`a* of writing altogether.

Then, when the Arabs rose to power, when they conquered cities and took possession of provinces; when they settled in al-Basra and al-Kufa, the State (*al-dawla*) needed writing. Then, they adopted the written word and they sought to practice and study it—making it pass from teacher to student and from generation to another. As a result, a high degree of excellence in writing was achieved. Writing became firmly established in al-Kufa and al-Basra, especially, where it reached a level degree of accuracy, but did not reach the desired limit of perfection. The Kufic script is widely known even in this time.

The Arabs, then, spread over all the regions and dynasties and opened (*iftatahu*) *Ifrīqiyya* (Tunisia; North Africa) and *al-Andalus* (Spain). The Abbasids penned (*ikhṭaṭṭa*) Baghdad, where different kinds of writing reached the limit of perfection, given the level of urbanization there—becoming the Home of Islam (*Dar al-Islam*) and the seat of the state (*markaz al-dawla*).

The status of writing in Baghdad differed from that in al-Kufa, in that the latter was influenced by improved forms (*ijādat al-rusūm*), beautiful sound (*jamāl al-rawnaq*), and brilliant narrative (*ḥusn al-riwā'*). This difference became established in many regions (*Amṣār*) when it was championed by Ali Ibn Muqla al-Wazir in Baghdad. He was followed in this respect by Ali Ibn Hilal, the author known as Ibn al-Bawwab. References to teaching writing stopped with him in the year 300 and beyond.

The forms of the written Baghdadi script moved further from the Kufic writing script, reaching a complete break (*al-mubāyana*). Then, the divergence increased afterwards, when al-Janabitha exerted maximum efforts to invent new forms and structures of writing, up to the time of the later scribes (*muta'akhkhirīn*) including Yaqut and al-Waliyy Ali al-`Ajami. The reference to authority stopped with them, before authority moved to Egypt where writing was somewhat different from the Iraqi writing system, which was taught to non-Arabs there (in Iraq); and appeared to be different or distinct from the writing systems developed by the people of Egypt.

The most known written form of Arabic was the Baghdadi script, followed by the Ifrīqī script, whose old form also has been known until this time, and which was close in form to the eastern script. Governing *al-Andalus* became influenced by the values of the Umayyads and that gave *al-Andalus* special character to their cities, their *ṣanā'i`*, and their writing systems. As a result, the Andalusian script stood out with its characteristic style known until our time.

The sea of urbanization flowed high in all Islamic states (*al-duwal al-islāmiyya*) in every region (*quṭr*). State power increased and markets of sciences thrived. Books were copied in excellent styles and covers. Palaces become full with these books and so were the governmental libraries—they were all filled with them in an incomparable way, causing people of all regions to compete for them.

Then, when the Islamic state system collapsed or became weak, the legacy of Baghdad became limited to lessons on the caliphate. Consequently, its position as center of calligraphy and writing actual sciences, all moved to Egypt and Cairo where the markets for these arts and sciences thrived until our time. There, teachers taught writing by known rules that govern the styles, shapes, and positions, making the learners well-prepared to produce excellent books based on scientific methods that made it[74] of the best quality.

The people of *al-Andalus*, on the other hand, dispersed in different regions after the fall of the Arab rulers, who were replaced by the Berber rulers. Moreover, the Christian nations defeated them, so they moved to *al-Maghrib* and the north African region (*Ifrīqiyya*) and that has been their state to this day. There, they collaborated in urban centers given their mastery of many *ṣanā'i`*. They attached themselves to the rulers who adopted their style of writing, making it dominant over the local African script, which become forgotten and unused. Some of these forgotten local scripts including the script of Qayrawan (*khaṭṭ al-qayrawān*) and the script of al-Mahdiyya, they were both forgotten when people had forgotten these two customs (*`awā'id*) and these two *ṣanā'i`*. As a result, all the scripts (*khuṭūṭ*) of the people of North Africa (*Ifrīqiyya*) became written in the Andalusian form (*al-rasm al-andalusī*) in Tunis and neighboring regions because of the existence of people who relocated there from the eastern parts of *al-Andalus*.

One script, however, survived and that is the one in the country of al-Jrid (southern Tunisia), because people of that region did not interact with writers from *al-Andalus* and they did not practice near them.

Since the Andalusian writers and calligraphers used to visit the capital city Tunis, the script of the people of *Ifrīqiyya* (Tunisia and parts of modern Algeria) thus became a representative of the Andalusian writing script and the best of all Andalusian scripts.

[74] Writing

However, when the shadow of the Almohad dynasty receded somewhat, and urban-living and the culture of luxury retrogressed with the retrogression of urbanization, writing also suffered a setback, and its forms deteriorated. The method of teaching writing was no longer known, due to corruption in its sciences and the decrease in urbanization. Traces of the Andalusian script remain there, though, a witness to what used to be there. As we have mentioned before, the existence of such traces is explained by the fact that, once *ṣanā'i`* take hold in an urban setting, it are difficult to fully erase the *ṣanā'i`*.

In the later Marinid Dynasty in Morocco, a kind of Andalusian script became established, because the Andalusians were close neighbors and the Andalusians who left *al-Andalus* soon settled in Fez. Once there, the Marinids employed them during all the days of their rule. However, in regions far from the seat of government and the capital of the realm, writing was not cared for, and it was forgotten as if it had never been known. The scripts (*khuṭūṭ*) used in *Ifrīqiyya* (Tunisia) and among the people of Maghrib (*maghribiyyīn*) were likely to be ugly and far from excellent. When books were copied, it was useless to look at them or study from them. Looking at them caused nothing but pain and trouble, because the texts were very corrupt and full of errors; and the letters were no longer well formed. Thus, they could be read only with some difficulty. As such, writing was affected like all the other *ṣanā'i`* by the decrease of urbanization (*ḥaḍara*) and the corruption of the State; and God rules, and none can rescind his rule.

Professor Abu al-Hasan Ali Ibn Hilal, the renowned Baghdadi author (*al-khatīb al-Baghdādī al-shahīr*), who is known as Ibn al-Bawwab, wrote a poem in the *basīt* meter that rhymed with the r. In it, he mentions the *ṣinā`a* of writing and the matters with which it is connected. The poem belongs among the best things ever written on the subject. I thought I would republish it in this book so that those who want to learn the *ṣinā`a* of writing may benefit from it. It starts:

O you who want to master editorializing,

and feel comfortable with writing and drawing;

If your determination to writing is true,

pray that your lord make it easy for you;

Prepare any pen that is sharp,

strong, capable of fashioning elegant writing with *ṣinā`a* of ink;

If you propose to nib the calamus,

aim at calculating with the most average of assumptions;

Look at both ends of it and make its contours,

shaped by details and sharpened by preparation

Make its outline erect and straight,

free from unnecessary elongations and shortening;

And make the split precisely in the middle of it,

so that the spaces around it are equally adjusted;

once you have done all that carefully,

then turn all your attention toward the overall estimation;

Don't even think that I will reveal its secret,

for I am chary of its secret, the well-hidden secret.

But the total of what I would say is that,

it should be something between strokes and circles.

And store your tools in smoked ends,

submersed in vinegar or squeezed verjuice.

Add to it pigment that has been diluted,

with smallest parts of orpiment and camphor.

Once it has fermented, then select,

the clean, shining, pressed paper.

Then hold it, after cutting it with pressing tool so that,

It is free of crumpling and folding.

Then adopt imitation as your approach, patiently,

what is hoped for is only secured by those who are patient.

Begin it on the wooden board, selecting for it

a resolution that keeps it free from haste.

Do not be ashamed of ugliness that you draw

in your first draft and outline;

The matter is hard at first but becomes easy,

for all difficult matters become easy.

Once you achieve what you hoped for,

you will become a person of joy and skill.

Therefore, thank your God and follow what pleases Him,

for God answers the prayers of every grateful person.

And wish that your palm's fingers would draw,

only what is good is left behind in the house of pride.

For all acts a person does, he will be reunited with them tomorrow,

at the conclusion of much efforts, a book documenting the acts will be published.

Know that the written work is an expression of saying and speaking. The same way saying and speaking express what is in the soul and what is on the mind. Therefore, both must be clear in what they express. God says: "He created the human; taught him clarifying. "*khalaqa al-insān, `allamahu al-bayān*." This would include clarifying (*bayān*) all the facts (*adilla*).

Therefore, the improved written word is perfected when its meaning (*dalālatuh*) is clear by indicating clearly the required letters and their proper arrangement and shapes—each letter is distinct from the other, except where connections of letters within a word is conventionally followed. This may apply to letters that are conventionally non-connected, the alif when it is the first letter of a word; or the letters *al-rā', al-zay, al-dal, al-dhal*, etc., which are governed by a different rule were they are to be at the end of the word, and so on and so forth.

Some later scribes (*kuttāb*) adopted a style that connects words to one another or the omission of known letters; as per their convention. But such practices are known amongst them and may appear to be foreign (*ista`jama*) to other scribes. However, there are the record-keepers of the sultans and the registry of judges; they appear to have used this practice to the exclusion of other scribes for they have to write a great deal, and they are known for their writing style, and many people connected with them know their code. When they write to others who do not know their code, they cannot use it and have to try to write as clearly as possible.

Otherwise, their writing might as well be a foreign language script (*al-khaṭṭ al-a`jamī*). It would be in the same category with it[75] in as much as both types of writing, the code and non-Arabic writing, are not generally agreed upon by conventional usage. There is no real excuse for writing in code, except in the case of officials of the government's tax and army offices. In these cases, they are required to conceal the information from the people, for these are government secrets that must be kept secret. Therefore, they used a very special code among themselves, which is like a puzzle. It makes use of the names of perfumes, fruits, birds, or flowers to indicate the letters, or it makes use of forms different from the accepted forms of the letters. Such a code is agreed upon by the correspondents between themselves, in order to be able to convey their thoughts in writing.

It might be the case that skillful secretaries, though not the first to invent a certain code and with no previous knowledge of it, nonetheless find rules for deciphering it through combinations that they develop for the purpose with the help of their abilities, and which they call "solving the puzzle (decoding)." Well-known writings on the subject are available for the people to access. And God is Knowing, Wise.

[75] Language

31. On Writing and Recordkeeping

In the past, interest in scientific reports and records, including copying, editing, and binding, was there because of the effects of urbanization and increased size of the State (*ḍakhāmat al-dawla*). Today, all that is gone because the State is gone and because settlements in urban centers have decreased compared to what they used to be during the Islamic rule that generated a sea of written records in Iraq and *al-Andalus*. The existence of written records and books, or the lack thereof, is connected to expansive urban living, State control over large areas, and funded markets for such products. These conditions make it possible for writing scientific records and registries, and people were interested in transferring them across time and across places. Therefore, they were copied and bound in the form of books.

Thus was born the *ṣinā`a* of recordkeeping (*wirāqa*) handled by record-keepers (*al-warrāqūn*) whose job was to copy, correct, edit, bind, and to do all other book-related matters—a *ṣinā`a* especially present in countries (*Amṣār*) with largely populated urban centers (*`aẓīmatu al-`umrān*).

At first, the function of the registries was to replicate scientific knowledge, monographic treatises, and governmental correspondences. The documents were written on parchment specially prepared from animal skins, because of the abundance of luxury and the limitedness of writing during the early days of the Islamic rule as we recall it. Moreover, government documents and official cables were few in number. Therefore, the record-keepers of that time limited themselves to writing on parchment as a form of respect for what is being written down, and as an inclination to produce correct and accurate records.

Then, the sea of interest in writing and publishing had risen and the production of governmental documents increased in number, making the supply of parchment insufficient. As a solution, al-Fadl Ibn Yahya recommended the manufacturing of paper (*ṣinā`at* *al-kāghit*). He then proceeded to manufacture paper and on it he wrote down the governmental documents and official notices (*sukūk*). After that, people used paper sheets for government and scholarly writings, and the manufacture of paper reached a high degree of quality.

The concern of scholars and the interest of government agents, then, focused on accuracy in scholarly writings and the establishment of their correctness with the help of a chain of transmitters leading back to their writers and authors, because that is the most important element in establishing a correct and accurate document. Statements are thus connected back to those who made them, and decisions in religious questions (*fatwā*), are connected back to the authority (*mujtahid*) who decided in accordance with them and were able to authenticate them by means of independent judgment (*ijtihād*).

Should a text not be corrected by connecting it through a chain of transmitters (*isnād*) going back to the person who wrote that original text, the statement or decision in question cannot be properly ascribed to its alleged author. This has been the procedure of scholars and experts in sciences in all times, generations, and horizons.

The usefulness of the *ṣinā`a* applicable to Hadith became limited to the chain of transmitters only. In that, its main achievement was the determination of level of reliability, as being sound (*ṣaḥīḥ*), good (*ḥasan*), continuous (*mursal*), interrupted (*maqṭū`*), ended (*mawqūf*), or made-up (*mawḍū`*) by examining the traditions' chain of transmitters (*isnād*). The cream of this endeavor has been churned in the principal collections of Hadith and other books including law (*fiqh*) and legal judgements (*fatwā*) works as well as official records and scientific registries and their connections to the authors (*isnād*), which make their citation (*naql*) and referencing valid.

These writings have had a paved path in the East and in *al-Andalus*, governed by clear rules and methods. Consequently, we find the copies of the registries from those times in those regions to be the most accurate, precise, and correct. People everywhere possess old copies attesting to the perfection previously reached in this respect to this day. People of the peripheries, regions on the edge of the Islamic territories, have handed them down and took good care of them.

However, these writings (*rusūm*), at the present time, disappeared altogether in *al-Maghrib* (Morocco) and people in this country did not have access to them because the *ṣinā`a* of writing, proofing, citation, and referencing were interrupted there as the result of the decrease in population of urban centers and their reversion to rural living style.

Consequently, the main collections (*ummahāt*) and registries were written by hand by Berber students. They would replicate them into such foreign bound volumes due to bad handwriting, widespread corruption, and poor binding work. Such materials are, then, inaccessible to those who examine them, providing no benefit whatsoever, except in some rare cases.

This condition affected the process of formal legal determination (*fatwā*), since most of the cited sayings are not connected to leaders of the school of jurisprudence. Rather, they are derived from the registries (*dawāwīn*) despite their unreliable conditions.

This has also affected the attempts of some leaders to write books. Leaders who knew little of writing and about related *ṣanā'i`* that help attain its purposes. Only faint remnants of *ṣinā`a* of writing had remained in *al-Andalus*, and even that is about to disappear. In fact, acquiring knowledge (*`ilm*) almost totally disappeared in *al-Maghrib*. "And God overrides all by His command."

To this day, we now hear that the *ṣinā`a* of transmission (*riwāya*) still exists in the East. Those interested in the study and correction of registries there may easily do so because of the existence of a competitive, well-funded markets of sciences and *ṣanā'i`* there, as we shall mention later on. However, the script that was left out of improvement endeavors there is the foreign script. In

Egypt, the art of writing was as corrupt as that in *al-Maghrib* or worse. And God, Almighty knows best, and by Him one attains success.

32. On the *Ṣinā`a* of Singing

This *ṣinā`a* encompasses musical composition (*talḥīn*), which is the fragmentation of metered poems (*al-shi`r al-mawzūn*) into ordered potions that are known when each is sounded out, it would turn in to a tune (*naghma*).

The tunes are then composed (*tu'allaf*), strung together in known portions that pleases the listener due to the harmony (*tanāsub*) it generates and the sounds it makes.

The science of music has already shown that sounds create harmony through proportions, where a sound can be one-half, one-quarter, one-fifth, or one-eleventh of another sound. These differences in proportions among the sounds that reach the ear transform them from simple sounds into composition of sounds. Not every composition is pleasant to listen to. Rather, a pleasant composition must have specific arrangement of portions of sounds, which have been enumerated and discussed by music scholars, as is mentioned in the proper place.

The *talḥīn* of tunes may be coupled with other bits of sound derived from solids and are produced by either beating or blowing into instruments used for this purpose. The use of such music instruments enhances the experience of listening, adding more pleasure to it. Today, in *al-Maghrib*, for instance, there are many instruments including a pipe-wind (*mizmār*), they call *shabbāba*, which is a hollow reed with a number of holes on the sides. When one blows into it, it would make a sound.

The sound escapes from the hollow of the reed through these holes. The sound can be stopped by placing the fingers of both hands upon these holes in conventionally accepted ways. This creates the proper intervals between the sounds and also combines them harmoniously. As a result, they are pleasant to listen to when one hears them, because of the harmony we have mentioned.

Another instrument similar to the *mizmār* is one called *al-zulamī*. It has the form of a reed, with two wooden parts carved hollow, hollow but not round, because it is made of two pieces put together. It also has a number of holes. One blows into it through a small, connected reed which directs the wind to the holes. This produces a high-pitched tune. The fingers are placed on the holes and the sounds are thus produced in the same way as on the *shabbāba*.

One of the best wind instruments at this time is *al-būq*. This is a trumpet of copper brass which is hollow, one cubit long, widening toward the opening, the diameter of estimated to be less than the palm of a hand in width. It has the form of a nibbed pen (*qalam*). Using it involves blowing into it through a small reed, which conveys the wind from the mouth into it. The sound comes out compact and loud. It also has a number of holes, and makes a harmonious tune with a pleasant effect, which is produced in the same way as in the aforementioned instruments, by placing the fingers on the holes.

Among these instruments, there are also the string instruments. They are all hollow. They may have either the shape of a section of a sphere, like, for instance, the *barbiton* and the *rebec*, or a square shape, such as the *qanun*. The strings are placed upon the surface of the instrument. They are tied at the head to pegs that can be turned, so that it is possible to tighten or loosen the strings as required, by turning them. The strings are either plucked with another piece of wood or played with a string fastened between the two ends of a bow that passes over the strings of the instrument after it had been waxed with wax and *kandar*. Sounds are produced through lightening the pressure of the hand that guides the bow over the strings, or through transferring the bow from one string to another. Moreover, in all string instruments, the fingers of the left hand can be used to beat or pluck the ends of the strings. Thus, there originate harmonious, pleasant sounds. Moreover, brass kettles may be beaten with sticks, or pieces of wood may be beaten against each other in a harmonious rhythm. This creates a feeling of pleasure as the result of the music one hears. Let us explain to you the cause of the pleasure resulting from singing (*ghinā'*).

As has been established in the proper place, pleasure is the attainment of something that is sensed and that is agreeable. Such a thing, in sensual perception, can only be a quality. If such a quality is proportionate and agreeable to the person who senses it, then it is pleasant. If it is repugnant to them or discordant, then it is painful.

Agreeable foods are those whose quality corresponds to the temper and composition (*mīzāj*) of the sense of taste. The same applies to agreeable sensations of touch. Agreeable smells are those that correspond to the temper of the vaporous cordial spirit, because that spirit is what perceives and receives them through the medium of the sense of smell.

Thus, aromatic plants and flowers smell better and are more agreeable to the spirit, because heat, which is the temper of the cordial spirit, is preponderant in them.

Agreeable sensations of vision and hearing are caused by harmonious arrangement in the forms and qualities of the things seen or heard. This impresses the soul as harmonious and is more agreeable to it.

As to the seen things: If an object of vision is harmonious in the forms and lines given to it in accordance with the matter from which it is made, so that the requirements of its particular matter as to perfect harmony and arrangement are not disregarded, that being the meaning of beauty and loveliness whenever these terms are used for any object of sensual perception, that object of vision is then in harmony with the self (*nafs*) that perceives it, and the self, thus, feels pleasure as the result of perceiving something that is agreeable to it. Therefore, we find the lovers (*al-`ashiqīn*) who are deeply in love express their extreme infatuation by saying that their souls (*arwāḥ*) are mixed (*imtizāj*) with that of their beloved. In this, there is a secret that you could understand if you are one of its seekers: the unity of origins (*ittiḥād al-mabda'*), in that, looking at someone else, and if you pay attention, you will see that between you and them there is a unity of origins (*ittiḥādan fi al-badā'a*).

This is true in the universe: that is, in other words, the existence (*al-wujūd*) creates commonality among existent things, as philosophers contended. One would seek the proximity of that which is perfect so that one may acquire perfection for themselves. Rather, the self would tend to then leave the myth and enter into reality, which is unity of origins and existence.

Since the thing most likely to help the human being attain perfection (*yudrik al-kamāl*) in ideal proportions is the human form (*shakluh al-insānī*), his ability to attain perfection in beauty and goodness in their writings and sounds is one of the goals (*madārik*) that is closest to his nature (*fiṭratih*). Therefore, every human (*insān*) has burning desire to seek out the good in what can be seen or heard, driven by their nature (*fiṭra*).

Goodness (*ḥusn*) in what is heard (*al-masmū`*) is when the sounds are harmonious and not discordant. That is so for sounds has modes of expression including the whisper, the loud, the soft, or the strong, the vibration, the pressure, and so on.

The existence of harmony (*al-tanāsub*) in it is what endows the thing with goodness (*al-ḥusn*). This can be achieved through:

Firstly, the sound cannot be emitted all at once, but gradually (*bi-tadrīj*); and then answered the same way to the similar sound. In fact, the change must mediate the two sounds moderately. For illustration, observe how linguists pronounce the compositions of letters that are distant or connected and where the sounds are produced. This belongs to the same category.

Secondly, the sounds must have harmonious intervals, as was mentioned at the beginning of this section. The transition from a sound to its one-half, its one-third, or some other fraction of it, must take place in a harmonious manner according to the rules established by the masters of the *ṣinā`a* of music. When the sounds are harmonious with regard to their qualities, as has been mentioned by the masters of the *ṣinā`a* of music, such sounds would be agreeable and pleasant.

Some of the harmony (*tanāsub*) may be a simple one and it would imprinted (*maṭbū`*) in many people. As such, they do not need any teaching or *ṣinā`a* for it that would be needed for them to acquire it. The same way, we find people enabled by nature for the meters of poetry (*mawāzīn shi`riyya*), the rhythms of the dance, and similar things. The common people call such an aptitude to music *al-midmār*.

Many Qur'an readers are of this kind. In reciting the Qur'an, they know well how to modulate their voices, as if they were blow-horns (*mazāmīr*). Their recitation causes emotion through the beauty of their performance and the harmony of their tunes.

Some of the harmony may also achieved by combination. Not all human beings are equal in their knowledge of it, nor are they all equally able by nature to practice it, if they know it. This is composition (*talḥīn*), the purview of the science of music, as we will explain later when we address the topic of sciences.

Malik, *raḥimahu allāh*, disapproved of the musical reciting the Qur'an (*al-qirā'a bi-al- talḥīn*), whereas al-Shāfi'ī, *radiya allāhu ta`āla `anh*, permitted it. Here it should be made clear that the dispute is not over the composition using musical manufactured instruments, for there is no dispute concerning its prohibition.

The art of singing is something entirely unconnected with the Qur'an. Singing (*ṣinā`at al-ghinā'*) is totally distinct from the Qur'an in every way, for reading and performing require some sound to pronounce the letters, not from the aspect of following the vowels in their respective locations and the amount of time the sound lasts (*madd*), be it long or short, and the alike.

Composition (*talḥīn*), too, requires a measure of sound, without it, it cannot happen for the purpose of harmony (*tanāsub*), which we indicated in relations to *talḥīn* and in the fact that one may negatively impact the integrity of the other when they conflict with each other.

The preference of recitation (*tilāwa*) is required to avoid change corrupting the narrative (*riwāya*), which is preserved in the Qur'an. Therefore, composition and performance cannot be applied in the Qur'an in anyway. What is implied here is the simple composition (*al-talḥīn al-baṣīṭ*) to which the person of tune is inspired to make naturally as we explained above, where they would resonate their voice in a way that will be understood by the expert in singing and the like, and that cannot happen in any way. What is meant is their disagreement (*ikhtilāf*) regarding the simple composition (*al-talḥīn al-baṣīṭ*), to which the composer (singer) would stumble upon on their own due their nature (*bi- ṭab`ih*); as we explained; whereby they would resonate their voice in proportions that would be understood by those who know singing and the alike. And this is not allowed as decreed by Malik. This is the heart of the dispute.

The obvious aim is the keeping of the Qur'an free from all of this and this is the intent of Imam Malik, *raḥimahu allāh ta`āla*. This is the case because the Qur'an is a locus of mindfulness (*khushū`*), for reminding people of death and what is after death. The Qur'an is not a tool of pleasure through the enjoyment of good voices, and this applies to the recitations by the Companions, *radiya allāhu `anhum*, as reported to us in our traditions.

As to the statement by the Prophet, *ṣallā allāhu `alayhi wasallam*, that "he was given a mizmar from the *mazāmīr* of the clan of David;" it does not refer to repeating and composing (*tardīd wa-talḥīn*). Rather, it refers to a beautiful voice, a clear pronunciation in reciting the Qur'an, and a clear distinction in the articulation and enunciation of the letters.

Since we have mentioned the meaning of singing, it should be known that singing takes place in densely populated urban centers when it becomes abundant and people start to look for what they want and move beyond what they need, and then to the luxuries, and become skilled and selective in producing it—thus this *ṣinā`a* is born. For such *ṣinā`a* will not be sought except by those who have fulfilled all their important necessary needs, including securing an income and providing a home, and the like. Therefore, only those who freed themselves to pursue the ways of pleasure, competing in seeking it and through artistic endeavors.

Before Muslims took over, the non-Arab States (*sulṭān al-`ajam*) enjoyed a vast interest in this, making it widely available in countries and cities. These rulers used to be infatuated with this to the extent that the kings of Persia took great interest in the people of this *ṣinā`a* and they gave them great power in their state, including the kings attending their performances and singing with them. This remained the practice among the *`ajam* to this day, in every horizon of their horizons and in every kingdom of their kingdoms.

The Arabs, on the other hand, first they had the art of poetry. They composed a kind of speech consisting of equal parts of harmonious proportions connected to the number of voweled[76] and silent letters (*mutaḥarrik, sākin*). They would detail speech in these sections to a high level of detail, each part is independently treated for attention not extended to the next part, and they would call this *al-bayt* (verse). It is agreeable to nature first by its division into parts, then by the harmonious arrangements of its parts at the ends and beginnings, and then by the fact that it conveys the intended meaning and uses expressions conforming to that meaning. This genre became special compared to other speech. It was honored due to its special form and harmony. They made poetry the registry of their history, their governance, and their honor. And they made it the touchstone of their natural ability for expressing themselves correctly, choosing the best methods (*asālīb*) and they continued to do so.

The harmony resulting from the division of speech into parts, and into an equal number of voweled and silent parts, is just

[76] A consonant that has a vowel associated with it

one small drop in the ocean of sound harmony, as is well known from the books on music.

However, the Arabs did not know anything except poetry, because at that time, they practiced no science and knew no *ṣināʿa*; for rural-living was their dominant style of living.

Those who took care of camels sang when they drove their camels; young men sang when they were in their solitude (*khalwatihim*); and they repeated sounds and hummed them. When such humming was applied to poetry, it was called singing; and when it was *tahlīl* or some kind of recitation, it was called *taghbīr* (spelled with *ghayn muʿjama* and *bā' muwaḥḥada*). Abu Isḥāq al-Zajjāj explained this word as being derived from *al-ghadbīr*, that is, which means the enduring (*al-bāqī*) that is, the affairs of the hereafter.

The Arabs, when they sang, they often affected a simple harmony between the modes, as was mentioned by Ibn Rashiq at the end of *kitāb al- umda*, and by others. They used to call it *al-sinād*. Most Arabic music was in the light (*khafīf*) rhythm that is used for dancing and marching, accompanied by drums and *mizmar*. It causes emotion and makes the serious-minded feel light. The Arabs called that *al-hazaj*. All these are simple types of compositions and among their earliest. It is not far-fetched to assume that they can be grasped by nature without any teaching, as is the case with all simple *ṣanā'iʿ*. This was the case among the Arabs during their rural living stage and during the *jāhiliyya* period.

Then, when Islam had arrived, and when the Arabs took possession of all the realms of the world, they defeated the non-Arab states and took their power, while still tethered to rural-living, but empowered by strength of the religion and its emphasis on abandoning inactivity (*al-farāgh*) and anything that does not benefit the religion or making a living, then, they moved away from that to some extent. In their opinion, only the cadenced recitation of the Qur'an and the humming of poetry, which had always been their way and custom, were acceptable pleasurable things.

Then, luxury and prosperity came to them, because they obtained the spoils of the nations. Then, they came to lead splendid and refined lives and to appreciate leisure and the enjoyment of downtime. Singers left the Persian and Byzantine lands to settle in Hijaz. They became clients (*mawali*) of the Arabs. They all sang accompanied by lutes, lyres, and flutes. The Arabs heard their compositions of sounds, so they composed to these compositions their own poems.

Nashit al-Farlsi, Tuways, and Sa`ib Khathir, a client of `Abdallah Ibn Jafar, all made their appearance in the city of Madina. They heard the poems of the Arabs and composed it (*laḥḥanūh*) magnificently. Consequently, they became famous. From them, Ma`bad and his generation of singers, as well as Ibn Shurayj and his equally talented artists all learned from them. Continuous and gradual progress was made in the *ṣinā`a* of singing until the days of the `Abbasids, during which time the *ṣinā`a* of singing reached its perfection with Ibrahim Ibn al-Mahdi, Ibrahim al-Mawsili, Ibrahim's son, Ishaq, and Ishaq's son, Hammad. The rulers of these states in Baghdad became known and talked about and their courts are organizing musical sessions to this day. They indulged themselves playing and entertaining. They are adopting dancing equipment, including robes, sticks, and the poems to which they would move, hum, and dance. Other dancing equipment, called *al-karj*, was also used, which is a wooden figure resembling a saddled horse and is attached to robes that women would wear and make it look like they are mounting horses. They attack and withdraw and compete in skill with weapons and other games designed for parties, banquets, wedding parties, festivals, and other gatherings for leisure and entertainment. There were much of these activities in Baghdad and the cities of Iraq, and from there it spread to other cities and other regions.

Among the people of Mosul, there was a young man named Ziryab, who had learned from them how to sing and excelled at it, which made them jealous of him. So they sent him away to *al-Maghrib*. He joined al-Hakam Ibn Hisham Ibn Abd al-Rahman al-Dakhil, the *amīr* of *al-Andalus*. Al-Hakam honored him greatly. He even rode out to welcome him. He showered him with gifts, fiefs, and allowances. He gave him a place in his dynasty as one of his companions. The musical heritage Ziryab left in *al-Andalus* was transmitted down to the time of the era of factional rule (*azmān al-ṭawā'if*). In Sevilla (*ishbīliyya*), the *ṣinā`a* of singing was highly developed. After Sevilla had lost its affluence, the *ṣinā`a* of singing was transferred from there to the coast of *Ifrīqiyya* and *al-Maghrib*. It spread over the cities there though a remnant of it was left there, despite decreased urbanization and receding power of its states.

This *ṣinā`a* of singing and music is the last of the *ṣanā'i`* attained in settled urban centers (*``umrān*), for it is complementary (*kamāliyya*) but to no other occupation in all of the occupations except the occupation of downtime and joy (*al-farāgh wa-'l-faraḥ*). And it is the first to be interrupted in settled urban centers when urbanization falls off tracks and declines. And God knows More.

33. On the Fact that *Ṣanā'i`*, Especially Writing and Calculus, Endow its Masters with a Sharp Mind (*`aql*)

We have already mentioned in the book that the speaking self in the human being exists by force (*bi-'l-quwwa*). Its transformation from force-based into action-based (*al-fi`l*) takes places through the renewal of sciences and discoveries through senses first. Then, what is acquired through the force of abstract thinking until it becomes discovery in actuality and pure intellect (*`aql maḥḍ*). Thus, it becomes a spiritual self, at which point its existence then reaches completion.

For that to happen, it is necessary that each kind of learning and observation should provide it with added intellect (*`aqlan mazīdan*). The *ṣanā'i`* take precedence, that and the ability it endows in the person generates a scientific norm that benefits from such acquired ability. For this reason, experience provides intelligence; whereas the complete urban lifestyle provides intellect, for it is collected from a plurality of *ṣanā'i`* that may focus on taking care of the home, mixing with people of the same social category (*abnā' al-jins*), acquiring norms and ethics that govern such interactions, undertaking religious affairs, and considering the rules and conditions of the religious affairs. All these are norms and rules organized in some fashion to become sciences that result in an increase in intellect.

Writing is one of the *ṣanā'i`* most useful to increase intellect, for, unlike other *ṣanā'i`*, it includes sciences and theories. The explanation of this is that, through writing one moves from the written letters to the spoken words in one's mind; and from phrases made of words in one's mind to the meanings (*ma`ānin*) that are in the self (*fi al-nafs*)—thus a transition, initially, from proof to proof (*dalīl*), as long as it is ambiguous as written, but the self will build the ability always. This way, the self will gain the ability (*malaka*) to move from the proofs to the proven and that is the meaning of intellectual deliberation which allows one to gain unknown sciences, which in turn, allows one to develop an ability to exert the mind (*ta`aqqul*) that becomes added intellect (*ziyādat `aql*). With this added intellect, one would acquire a force (*quwwa*) of awareness and elegance in handling matters for one's being accustomed to transitioning.

For this reason, Kisra (Khosraw) said in his book when he saw them with that awareness and elegance (*al-fiṭna wa-'l-kays*), he said: "his *dīwān*, that is devils and insanity. They said: "and that is the origin of the derived word "*daywān*" for the people of writing (*ahl al-kitāba*).

To this category, one should add the master of calculations (mathematicians). The *ṣinā`a* of *ḥussāb* is the kind that is concerned with numbers, adding them and separating them. In it, one would need much deductive reasoning (*istidlāl*); one would then become accustomed to performing deductive and inductive reasoning and observation and that is the meaning of intellect (*`aql*). And God brought you out of your mothers' bellies knowing nothing, then He made for you hearing, seeing, and gut feelings (*af'ida*); yet you rarely express gratitude.

Glossary of Key Words and Concepts

`ajam – non-Arab(s)
`aql –mind, intellect
`aqlan mazīdan – added intellect
`aql maḥḍ – pure intellect
al-` āshiqūn/`āshiqīn – lovers
`awā'id – customs
`aysh – living, life
`āṣimat al-`umrān – urban center
A
abnā' al-jins – the same social category
ādamī – adjective from Adam, human
adilla – (pl.) facts, proofs
af`āl al-khayr – good deeds
af`āl al-sharr – bad deeds
af'ida – gut feelings
afkār – ideas
aghdhiya – foods, nutrients
ahl al-kitāba – the people of writing
ājur - bricks
ālāt – tools
al-amr al-ma`dūm – a void matter
a`māl*; sing. *`amal – human work
amrāḍ – diseases
amṣār – countries, regions
anṣār – Sponsors, supporters, people of Madina (city) who welcomed the Muslim migrants
aqwāt – foods
arwāḥ – souls
asālīb - methods
ashrāf – persons of eminence
aysar bi-kathīr – in much better financial conditions
azmān al- ṭawā'if (sing. *ṭā'ifa)* – factional rule
B
badan (al-) – the body
badw, badāwa – rural people, rural living
balgham (al-) - phlegm
bā' muwaḥḥada – be consolidated
baqā', baqā'uhum – endurance, their continued existence
bāqī (al-) – the enduring
barda (al-) – the introduction of new food to the food already in the stomach before it has been digested
bayān – clarifying
bayt (al-) - verse
binā' – building (as a trade)
bi-'l-quwwa – by force
bi-ṭab`ih – in (one's) nature
bi-'l-tadrīj – gradually
Būq (al-) – brass instrument

C
D
*dafa`a;* (daf`)– to push, pay; pushing, paying
ḍakhāmat al-dawla – greatly increased size of the State
dalālatuh – its meaning
dalīl - proof
damman `abīṭan – fresh blood
daqīq * – fine, grounded flour from wheat or barley
Dār al-Islām – Home of Islam; Land ruled according to Islamic teachings
dawāwīn - registries
dawla (al-)– the State
dawla (al-) al-umawiyya – the Umayyad State
dawlatayn – two separate states
dhakhīra – reserve, store
dhirā` - cubit, standard/unit for measuring length
dhull – humiliation
ḍarūrīyyāt – necessary things
duwal – nation-states
duwal (al-) al-islāmiyya – Islamic states
E
F
fāqid al-jāh – one who lacks social standing, he who lacks prestige
fā`il mukhtār – select agency
falḥ – agriculture
faqr – poverty
al-farāgh – downtime; emptiness, void
faraḥ (al-)– joy

fasidat – it became corrupted
fatwā – religious decree, legal judgement, decision in religious questions
fi al-akthar – in most cases
fi`l – actually, action-based
fikr – think, abstract thinking
fikriyya – intellectual
filāḥa – agriculture
fiqh – law
fiṭna (al-)– awareness
fiṭra – natural state, nature
G
ghalā' – high price
ghalaba – dominance
ghāli – expensive
ghayn mu`jama – anglicized/foreign pronunciation of the letter (ghayn)
ghazl – spinning yarn
ghinā' – singing
H
ḥarr (al-) al-gharīzī – natural enzymes/acids
Ḥadīth – the Tradition of the Prophet/Sunna
haḍm – digestion
ḥaḍāra (al-)– civilization
ḥaḍḍ – luck
ḥarr (al-) al-gharīzī – natural enzymes/acids
hālik (al-) – the deceased
ḥarām – proscribed, blameworthy
ḥarāra (al-) al-gharīziyya – instinctive heat, natural heat, body generated heat
ḥasan – good (adjective)
ḥawalāt/aḥwāl al-aswāq – market conditions
hawānan – diminutive
hayākil – structures
ḥayawān – animal
ḥayawānāt (al-) al-`ujum – nonspeaking animals
hazaj (al-)– music in a light rhythm used for dancing and marching, accompanied by drums and mizmar, which causes emotion and makes people feel light
ḥidāda – ironsmithship
ḥimya – hunger
ḥiyāka – tailoring, knitting, spinning
ḥūt – fish, large fish
ḥubūb (al-)– grains
ḥummā (al-)– fever
ḥummiyyāt – fevers
ḥuqūq – laws; rights
ḥussāb – person who are skilled in arithmetic calculations
ḥusn - goodness
ḥusn al-riwā' – brilliant narrative
I
iḍāfī – added value
ifranj – Frankian (countries)
Ifrīqiyya – the north African region
iḥtikār – hoarding
ijādat al-khaṭṭ – proficient in writing
ijādat al-rasm – proficient in making forms, drawing
ijtihād – exertion of independent reasoning
ikhṭaṭṭa – he penned
ikhtilāf – disagreement
ilhām – inspirational birth, inspiration
`ilm – knowledge
`ilm al- ṭabī`a – natural sciences
imāra – political leadership, governing
imtizāj – mixed
inqirāḍ – extinction
inqiṭā` - interruption
insān – human being
Ishbīliyya - Sevilla
isnād – chain of transmitters, connections to the authors
ista`jama – appear to be foreign, one behaves like non-Arabs
istidlāl – deductive reasoning
istirthāl – humility
istiṭāla – overwhelm
ittiḥād al-mabda',– the unity of origins
J
jāh – social standing, rank
jāhiliyya – the time before Islam emerged
jalā' – leaving
jamāl al-rawnaq – beautiful sound
jibilla – the ability to think

jundiyya – military
jur'a – initiative
K
kamāl – perfection
kamāliyya – complementary
kāmil al-ma`rifa – of complete knowledge
al-karj – dancing equipment that is a wooden figure resembling a saddled horse, attached to robes that women wear to make it look like they are riding horseback
kasb – earned income, earnings
kaymus – chyme
al-kays – elegance
khafīf – light
khalwa – solitude
khamr - wine
kharāb – ruin
khaṣāṣa – need
khaṭṭ – written word, writing
al-khaṭṭ al-ḥumayrī – Himyarite script
khaṭṭ al-qayrawān – Qayrawān script
al-khaṭṭ al-a`jamī – foreign language script
khawāṣṣ – the select segments of society
khayr – good
khayr kathīr – much good, lots of good
khild – mixture
khiyāṭa – tailoring
khuḍū` - subservience; subordinate
khuluq – character
khushū` - mindfulness
khuṭūṭ – scripts
khuṭūṭihim – (their) writings
kibar – aloofness
kils – quicklime
kitāb – book
kitāba – writing; authoring
kittān – cloth (material); Berber dialect: a fine cloth such as cashmere[77]
kuttāb – scribes
L
laḥḥana – to compose (music)
M
madd – the lengthening of a sound
ma`ādin – precious metals
ma`āni – meanings
ma`āsh, ma`āsh –making a living
ma`āsh al-rafah – luxury living
madārik – goals
madhalla – intimidation
madhhab – practice; a way of doing things
madhmūma – ill-spoken-of
mafād - benefit
al-Maghrib – Morocco
maghribiyyīn – people of Maghrib
majānan – free
makāsib – earnings
malaka, malakāt – ability, abilities
malakātih – development of (his) ability
manāfi` - benefits
maqatahu al-nās – people would hate him, people would have disdain for him
maqt – hate, dislike
maqṭū` - interrupted
ma`rifa – knowledge
markaz al-dawla – seat of the state
mashyakhat al-maghrib – the learned community of the Maghrib
al-masmū` - that which is heard
maṭāmīr, sing. *maṭmūr* – cellars, underground holes *
maṭbū` - imprinted
maṭbūkh – boiled food
mawqūf – ended
mawāli – clients
mawāzīn shi`riyya –meters of poetry
mawḍū` - made-up
mawlūd – newborn (noun)
mazāmīr – blow-horns
al-midmār – aptitude for music
miqdām – forthcoming

[77] There are two possible meanings for the translation of *kittān* in Ibn Khaldun's work. Within the Berber dialect, this word is general, referring to all cloth materials. The technical meaning in standard Arabic, however, refers to a specific kind of cloth, potentially cashmere.

miṣr –country or region
Miṣr - Egypt
mīzāj – composition
mizmār – pipe-wind
mubāyana – (complete) break
muftaqir – lacks, is unequipped
mughtarrīn – falsely thinking
mujtahid – authority (as a person), informed, learned thinker
mukammil – making something full, complete
mukāsaba – mutual earning
mukāyasa – cunning
muktasabāt - earnings
mulk – royal affairs
munashshita li-'l-arwāḥ – energizing to the spirits
mursal – continuous
murū'a (or *muruwwa*)- chivalry
muṣṭani`īn – pretenders
mutaḥarrik – voweled letter
muta'akhkhirīn – later (scribes)
mutaraffi`īn – high regard for oneself

N

al-nafs – the self
nafsā' – woman in labor
nafsih – same kind
naghma - tune
nahb – usurped
naql – citation, copying,
nasj – weaving
naw` gharīb – curious type
nijāra – carpentry
nuqsān – imperfection, diminution

O

P

Q

qābila – midwife
qahr – force
qalam – pen
qīma – value derived from basic goods or activities
qinya – value added through work
al-qirā'a bi-al-talḥīn – the musical reciting of the Qur'an
qudra qadīma – perpetual power
qumāsh – fabric
qūt – energizing materials, that which empowers the human body, food
qutn – cotton
quṭr – region
quwwa – potential, energy, force
quwwa nafsāniyya – force of the souls

R

rafh – comfort
raḥim – womb
rakhīṣ – cheap
al-rasm al-andalusī – the Andalusian form, script
ribḥ – gain
riwāya – transmission, narrative
rizq – subsistence
al-riyāḍa – sports
riyāsh – wealth
al-rūḥ al-ḥayawānī – the animal spirit
rujūliyya –masculinity
rukhṣ – cheapness (price)
rusūm – writings, shapes, drawings

S

sabiqat– instilled first
safahan – dishonest
safrā' – yellow bile
safsafa – nonsense
Ṣaḥāba – Companions (of the Prophet)
ṣaḥīḥ – sound, correct, true
sākin – inhabitant
sākin – silent letter
sawdā' – black bile residue
sa`y – effort, efforts
shabbāba – Moroccan wind instrument
shahwa – desired
shakhṣ – individual
shakluh al-insānī – his human form
shāri` - Lawgiver
sharr yasīr – little bad, small harm
shi`r mawzūn – metered poems
ṣibgha – mark
ṣibgha – lifestyle, color (figurative)
sikka – plowshare
shimam – high view of oneself
sila` - merchandises, goods
ṣinā`a – manufacturing (verbal noun)
ṣinā`a/ṣanā'i` - (sing./plur.) human work applied to specific materials, doing something, skill

ṣināʿat al-ghināʾ – singing
ṣināʿat al-kāghiṭ – paper manufacturing
subḥāna (allāh)– acknowledgement of God
ṣūf - wool
sukūk – official notices, checks
Sulṭān al-ʿajam – non-Arab powers
sunbul – ears (as of corn or wheat)
sunna – system
T
taʿaqqul – exert the mind
ṭabīb – medical doctor
ṭabiya – foundation, walls
tahlīl – a kind of chant
takarrarat – repeated
ṭalāq – freeing something or someone, or increasing something
talḥīn – musical composition, composing
talḥīn baṣīt – simple composition
tamalluq – flattery
tanāsub – harmony
tanmiya – developing
tanmiyat al-māl – capital growth
tanqaridu al-dawla – extinction of the State
tanzīh – absolving
taqabbala – accepts (something)
taraffuʿ – dignity and aloofness, above others' levels, transcendence, thinking too highly of oneself
tardīd- – repeating
ṭawāʾif - sectarian
tawlīd – midwifery
ṭawwāb – brick-layer
ṭibb – medicine (as a trade)
tijāra – trade
tilāwa – recitation
tuʾallaf - composed
tujjār – merchants, traders
turāb – soil
U
ʿadwā – infection, contamination
ummahāt – collections
ʿumrān – settled urbanization
ʿʿumrān – settled urban centers
ʿumūm – the public
ʿuṣūr – ages
V
W
warrāqūn – record-keepers
waswasa – whispers (as in rumors)
wāziʿ - deterrent
wirāqa – booksmanship, bookbinding, record-keeping
wujūd – existence
X
Y
yakhḍaʿ - submit (oneself) to a subordinate status
yaḥqid - grudge
yarziq – subsistence (provided by God or anyone else)
yasar – ease
yastaṣghirūn – they belittle
yaʿsur – become difficult
yatawahham – he falsely believes
yudrik al-kamāl – attain perfection
Z
ẓāhir – obvious
zakā – alms-giving
zarʿ - crops, agricultural goods
ziyādat ʿaql – added intellect
zulamī – a type of wind instrument

---

* The asterisk indicates words specific to Maghrebi dialect. This is particularly important when translating Ibn Khaldun's works due to the fact that past translators have made errors due to not taking his use of this dialect into consideration.

Index

`Abbasid Caliphate, 102
`Abdallah Ibn Jafar, 102
`Abdullah Ibn Farrukh Abd al-Rahman Ibn Ziyid Ibn An`am, 79
`Ad, 52
`ajam (non-Arab) States, 51, 100
`ajam (non-Arabs), 51, 83, 100
Abbasid Empire, 82
Abdallah Ibn Abbas, 79
Abdallah Ibn Jad`an, 79
Abdullah Ibn Farrukh, 79, 80
Abu al-Walid al-Waqshi, 80
Abu Bahr Ibn al-'As, 80
Abu Bakr Ibn Abi Himayara, 80
Abu Sa`id Ibn Yunus, 80
Abu Umar al-Tala`anki Ibn Abu Abdallah Ibn Mufrij, 80
Abu1-Hasan al-Mlili, 38
Adam, 7, 62
added value, 3, 82
Adhwa, 52
agriculture, 2, 4, 6, 7, 13, 30, 39, 54, 55
Ali Ibn Hilal, 83, 85
Ali Ibn Hilal (Ibn al-Bawwab), 83
Ali Ibn Muqla al-Wazir, 83
Almohad Dynasty, 85
Almohads, **48**
Amalekites, 52
Anbar, al-, 79
animals, 1, 6, 31, 33, 63, 70, 73, 74, 75, 77
  animal skins, 90
  birds, 15, 46, 89
  fish, 63
  horsemanship, 6
  lion, 14
animals (domestic), 3, 5, 6, 16, 45, 46, 57, 69, 71
  bees, 6, 69
  camels, 51, 62, 101
  donkeys, **46**
  horses, 76, 102
  silkworms, 6
Apollonius, 63
Arabs (people), 51, 78, 79, 80, 82, 100, 101, 102
Aslam Ibn Sudra, 78
Avicenna, 70, 71
Baghdad, 82, 83, 84, 102
Baghdadis (people), 83, 85
Bahlul Ibn Ubayda al-Himyi, 80
Bahrain, 52
Basra, al-, 82
bath attendant, **46**
beauty, 54, 96, 97, 98
Berbers (people), 12, 51, 84, 92
biology, 22
bookbinding, 44, 46, 83, 85, 90, 92
Bukhari, al-, 30
butchery, 44, **45**, **46**
Byzantine Empire, 12, 102
Cairo, 13, 46, 84
carpentry, 44, 45, 53, 54, 58, 62, 63
China, 17, 51
chivalry, 41
Christian nations, 51, 84
cisterns, 59
class. *See* jāh
climate, 56, 57
cloth, 4, 31, 52, 64, 65
  cashmere, 64
  cotton, 64
  silk, 15
  wool, 15, 51, 64
codebreaking, 89
commerce. *See* trade
Companions of the Prophet Muhammad, 81, 99
Constantinople, 60
construction, **15**, **47**, **53**, **54**, 56, **57**, 58, **59**, **60**, **63**
cooking, **46**, **47**, **73**, **75**
Coptic Empire, 12, 17, 52
David, clan of, 99
desert, 36, 80
disease. *See* illness

divine intervention, 69
earnings (*kasb*), 1, 2, 3, 4, 7, 12, 13, 17, 19, 20, 21, 23, 24, 28, 29, 31, 39, 41, 49, 77, 100
East, the, 14, 36, 51, 83, 91, 92
economics
  demand, 35, 44, 45, 46, 47, 49, 50, 77
  market conditions, 3, 32, 35, 39
Egypt (*Misr*), 13, 17, 46, 48, 77, 80, 83, 84, 93
engineering, 60, 61, 63
entertainment, **46**, 47, 102
Euclid, 63
Fadl Ibn Yahya, al-, 90
Farabi, al- (philospher), 69, 71
Fez, 37, 85
flora, 3, 6, 55, 75, 89
  aromatic, 96
  crop, 31
  flowers, 89, 96
food, 37, 40, 45, 55, 57, 72, 73, 74, 75, 76, 96
  flour, 31, 39
  grain, 4, 39, 40, 55, 75
  honey, 6, 40
  sugar, 40
Frankian countries, 17
gambling, 8
Gothic dynasty, **48**
Greeks (people), 17, 52
Hadith, 16, 74, 91
Hajj, 65
Hakam Ibn Hisham Ibn Abd al-Rahman al-Dakhil, al-, 102
haram (proscribed), 3, 38
Harb Ibn Umayya, 78, 79
Hariri, al-, 7
Hermes, 66
Hijaz, 79, 102
Himyar (people), 52, 78, 79, 80
Hira, al-, 79
Hirah, al-, 78
Hood (prophet), 79
houses, 15, 30, 56, 57, 59, 62
human nature, 1, 7, 9, 22, 25, 69, 97, 98, 99, 100, 101
hunting, 6, 13, 65, 76
Ibn al-Abari, 80
Ibn al-Abbar, 79
Ibn Farrukh al-Qayrawani al-Qasi al-Andalusi, 79
Ibn Rashiq, 101
Ibn Shurayj, 102
Ibrahim al-Mawsili, 102
Ibrahim Ibn al-Mahdi, 102
Idris (prophet), 7, 66
Ifrīqiyya. *See* North Africa (*Ifrīqiyya*)
illness, 72, 73, 74, 75, 76
income. *See* earnings (*kasb*)
India, 17, 51
inheritance, 2, 16, 24
intelligence, 41, 104
investment, 4, 29
Iraq, 48, 78, 80, 83, 90, 102
Iraqis (people), 78, 83
Islamic civilization, 84, 90, 100, 101
Israelites (people), 52
Iyad (clan), 78, 79
jāh, 10, 13, 19, 20, 21, 22, 23, 24, 25, 26, 28, 33, 42, 82
jāhiliyya (era), 16, 101
Janabitha, al-, 83
jewelry, 16, 46
Jrid, al- (southern Tunisia), 84
Jurhum, 80
kasb. *See* earnings (*kasb*)
Khilljan Ibn al-Qasam, al- (scribe), 79
Kisra (Khosraw), 105
Kitab al- umda, 101
Kufa, al-, 82, 83
labor, 3, 13, 19, 20, 44, 49, 67
law, 6, 7, 13, 16, 20, 22, 28, 29, 30, 33, 42, 88, 91
leisure, 102
Levant, the, 17, 60
libraries, 83
luxuries, 4, 13, 43, 44, 45, 46, 47, 48, 50, 52, 62, 65, 75, 77, 78, 85, 90, 100, 102
ma`āsh*. *See* making a living (*ma`ash)
Ma`bad, 102
Madina, 30, 102
Madina Mosque, 60
Maghrib, al-, 12, 13, 17, 37, 46, 51, 84, 92, 93, 94, 102, 103
magic, 12, 14, 16, 46

making a living (*ma`ash*). *See* subsistence (*rizq*) or earnings (*kasb*)
Malik (Imam), 60, 79, 98, 99
Ma'mun, al-, 29
manufacturing, 7, 44, 90
Marinid Dynasty, 85
Marinids (people), 85
Marrakech, **48**
masculinity, 9
mathematics, 105
medicine, 54, 68, 69, 72, 74, 75, 76
  treatment, 24, 56, 68, 72, 74
metal, 16, 17
  copper, 16, 17, 95
  gold, 3, 16, 17
  iron, 16, 17, 59
  lead, 16, 17
  silver, 3, 16, 17
  tin, 17
metalwork, 44, 45, **46**
midwifery, 54, 67, 68, 69, 70
  birth, 105
military, **44**
morality
  ethics, 34, 41, 104
  goodness, 97
Morocco, 85, 92
Mosul, 102
Mu`tazila, 2
Mudar, al-, 80
Muhammad Ibn Musa Ibn al-Nu`man, 80
Mundhir, al- (dynasty and clan), 78
Mushaf (people), 81
music, 47, 94, 95, 97, 98, 101, 103
  barbiton, 95
  booq, al-, 95
  composition, 58, 94, 97, 98, 99, 100, 101, 102
  dance, 46, 47, 98, 101, 102
  harmony, 94, 97, 98, 100, 101
  humming, 101, 102
  mizmar, 94, 98, 99, 101
  musical instruments, 47, 94, 95, 98, 99, 102
  percussion, **46**, 95, 101
  qanun, 95
  rebec, 95
  shabbaba, 94, 95
  singing, 44, 46, 47, 54, 95, 98, 99, 100, 101, 102, 103
  zulamiyy, al-, 95
Nabataeans (people), 52
Nashit al-Farlsi, 102
Nile (river), 14
Noah, 63
  Noah's Ark, 63
North Africa (*Ifrīqiyya*), 12, 17, 82, 84, 85, 103
Oman, 52
painting, **46**, **50**
perfection, 24, 25, 43, 44, 45, 46, 48, 57, 60, 78, 81, 82, 88, 92, 97, 102
Persian Empire, 12, 17, 52, 100, 102
philosophy, 69, 97
plants. *See* flora
pleasure, 37, 65, 94, 95, 96, 99, 100, 101
plowshare, 30
poetry, 14, 15, 24, 44, 78, 79, 85, 94, 98, 100, 101, 102
political leadership, 7, 19
pottery, **47**
pre-Islamic times, 12, 61
printing, 54
profits. *See* earnings (*kasb*)
property, 2, 8, 10, 16, 60
Prophet Muhammad, 2, 30, 69, 72, 79, 81, 82, 99
Qal`at Ibn Hammad, **48**
Qayrawan, al- (city), **48**
Quds Mosque, 60
Qur'an, 98, 99, 101
  recitation, 98, 99, 101
Quraysh, 78, 79
recordkeeping, 14, 44, 88, 90, 91, 92
religion, 28, 101
  fatwa, 28, 91, 92
  religious affairs, 28, 104
rizq. *See* subsistence (*rizq*)
Roman Empire, 12, 51
romance, 96
Romans (people), 52
royalty, 9, 10, 14, 21, 23, 24, 26, 27, 30, 34, 40, 54, 56, 57, 60, 100
rural living, 7, 20, 45, 51, 55, 72, 78, 80, 92, 101
  rural dwellers, 30, 56, 62, 64, 65, 74, 75, 76, 77, 80

Sa`ib Khathir, 102
Salaf, 81
sana'i`, 1, 6, 23, 39, 43, 44, 45, 46, 47, 48, 49, 50, 51, 52, 54, 55, 56, 58, 59, 60, 63, 64, 65, 66, 70, 77, 78, 79, 80, 82, 83, 84, 85, 92, 101, 103, 104
Sanhajah, **48**
Satan, 18
savings. *See* earnings (*kasb*)
sciences, 44, 45, 54, 77, 82, 83, 84, 85, 90, 91, 92, 98, 104, 105
sculpture, **50**
self, the, 22, 26, 53, 77, 82, 96, 97, 104
servitude, 9, 10, 11, 57
Sevilla, 103
Shafi`i, al- (Islamic scholar), 98
Shaykh Abu Abdallah al-Abli, 37
ships, 63
shoemaking, 6, **45**
singing. *See* music (singing), *See* music
Slovanian countries, 17
social standing. *See* jāh
Spain (*al-Andalus*), 47, 48, 82, 83, 84, 85, 90, 91, 92, 102, 103
spinning, 64
sporting activities, 75, 76
State, the, 26, 27, 28, 35, 49, 52, 60, 82, 83, 85, 90
subservience, 24, 26
subsistence (*rizq*), 1, 2, 3, 4, 6, 9, 18, 20, 28, 36, 40, 49
Sudan, 36, 66
Sufyan Ibn Umayya, 78
Sultan Abu Sa`id, 37
Sunna, 76
Sunni Muslims, 2
Syria, 48, 80
Ta'if, al-, 78
Tababi`a (people), 52, 78, 79
Tababi`a Dynasty, 78
Tabi`un, 81
tailoring, 3, 6, **45**, **53**, 54, 64
Takmila, al-, 79, 80
tanning, **46**, 51
taxation, 6, 7, 9, 18, 38, 40
temper (archaic physiological), 75, 76, 96
Thamud, 52
theft, 2, 10, 15, 33, 34, 37, 41
trade, 3, 6, 7, 13, 31, 32, 33, 35, 39, 40, 41, 42
  export, 32, 35, 36
  hoarding, 6, 37
  import, 35, 36, 51
  merchants, 19, 20, 23, 31, 32, 33, 34, 35, 36, 39, 40, 41, 42
treasure hunting, 12, 13, 15, 17, 18
treatises, 90
  The Treatise of Hayy Ibn Yaqzan, 70
Tubabi`a, 78
Tunis, 84
Tunisia, **12**, **17**, **48**, **84**, **85**
Turks (people), 51
Tuways, 102
Umayyad Empire, **48**, 83
urban living, 4, 5, 12, 13, 28, 36, 44, 45, 46, 47, 48, 49, 51, 52, 54, 56, 57, 59, 62, 64, 65, 72, 75, 77, 78, 79, 80, 82, 83, 84, 85, 90, 92, 100, 102, 103, 104
  urban dwellers, 7, 23, 28, 30, 40, 55, 65, 74, 75, 77
urbanization, 4, 16, 17, 45, 46, 50, 52, 77, 78, 82, 83, 85, 90, 99, 103
Waliyy Ali al-`Ajami, al- (scribe), 83
water, 5, 6, 14, 56, 58, 59, 60, 63
wealth, 2, 3, 9, 10, 12, 13, 16, 17, 19, 20, 21, 25, 26, 28, 29, 33, 42, 45, 56, 82
weaving, 51, 64
wine, 38
wood, 3, 62, 63, 95, 102
writing, 6, 12, 24, 54, 77, 78, 79, 80, 81, 82, 83, 84, 85, 86, 88, 89, 90, 92, 93, 104, 105
  books, 14, 29, 48, 54, 63, 79, 80, 83, 84, 85, 88, 90, 91, 92, 101, 104, 105
  calligraphy, 50, 77, 84
  editing, 86
  narrative, 83, 99
  paper/parchment, 87, 90, 91
  pen, 78, 79, 86, 95
  publishing, 90
Yahya Ibn Muhammad Ibn Hashish Ibn Umar Ibn Ayyub al-maghafiri al-Tunsi, 80
Yaqut (scribe), 83
Yemen, 52, 79, 80

www.ingramcontent.com/pod-product-compliance
Lightning Source LLC
Chambersburg PA
CBHW010330030426
42337CB00026B/4884
* 9 7 9 8 8 8 8 2 3 0 0 1 5 *